TIMESAVER

Grammar

ACTIVITIES (PRE-INTERMEDIATE – INTERMEDIATE)

Teacher's reference key

A small clock on each page tells you approximately
how long each activity should take.

Small icons at the top of each page show
whether the activity is best suited to individual, pair or group work.

Individual

Pair

Group

D1438309

TIMESAVER

Grammar

ACTIVITIES (PRE-INTERMEDIATE – INTERMEDIATE)

Contents

Articles / Nouns

Adjectives and Adverbs

Connecting Ideas

Prepositions

Phrasal Verbs

Answers

Who Are You?

Complete the information about yourself by finishing the sentences.

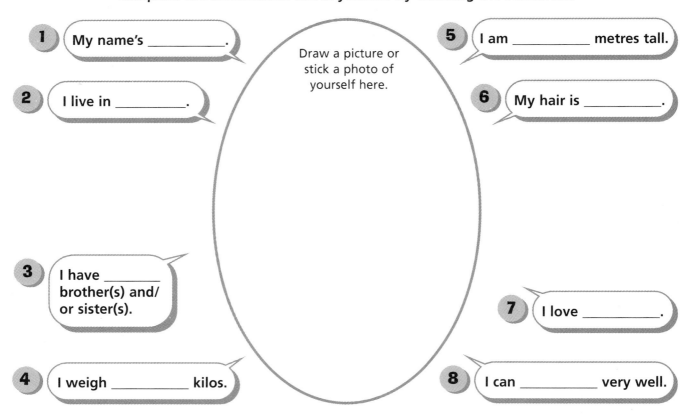

1 My name's _____ .

2 I live in _____ .

3 I have _____ brother(s) and/ or sister(s).

4 I weigh _____ kilos.

Draw a picture or stick a photo of yourself here.

5 I am _____ metres tall.

6 My hair is _____ .

7 I love _____ .

8 I can _____ very well.

Now, complete the same information about your best friend. This time you have to write whole sentences. Example:

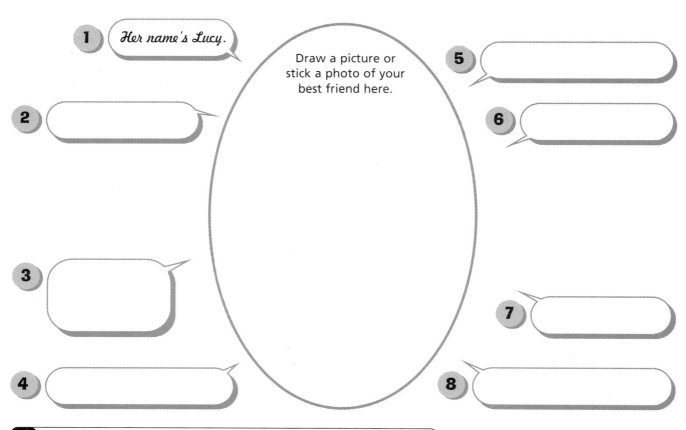

1 *Her name's Lucy.*

2

3

4

Draw a picture or stick a photo of your best friend here.

5

6

7

8

Unchanging World

The verbs in these fascinating facts are mixed up. Can you sort them out?

1

A koala bear **closes** for up to 22 hours each day. ☐

2

In the summer in the Arctic Circle, the sun never **travels**. ☐

3

An astronaut footprint on the surface of the moon **sleeps** for millions of years. ☐

4

The largest flower in the world is called a Rafflesia - it **lasts** up to 7 kilos and **loses** up to 1 metre across. ☐

5

If a lizard **drinks** its tail, it grows another one. ☐

6

In art galleries around the world, each visitor **measures** an average of 3 seconds in front of each painting. ☐

7

In baseball, when a pitcher **beats** a good ball, it **weighs** at about 160 kilometres an hour. ☐

8

An adult elephant **spends** about 225 litres of water every day. ☐

9

A snake never **throws** its eyes at any time. ☐

10

A human heart **sets** about 70 times a minute. ☐

Read the facts again...

✔ Put a tick next to the facts that you knew already.
★ Put a star next to the most interesting fact.
✗ Put a cross next to the least interesting fact.

You're Late!

It's Helen's birthday. She has invited a group of friends to go to the theatre to see a show. Her boyfriend, Rob, is late. Helen calls him on her mobile phone. Choose a verb from this box for each space in the conversation and put it in the present continuous. Use the pictures to help you

Each time you take a verb, write the letter next to it here to find the name of the show:

_ _ _   _ _ _ _   _ _ _ _

fall into	**n**
run out of	**g**
push	**n**
leave	**h**
sit	**e**
get on	**k**
run	**o**
go into	**i**
drive down	**i**
wait	**t**
get out	**l**

18.25 Where are you, Rob? Hurry up. We're all _____ at the theatre. The show starts in 35 minutes.

Sorry, Helen. I _____ the football club now. The football match finished very late but don't worry, my dad's promised to give me a lift.

18.30 Hi! I _____ in my dad's car – but there's a traffic jam.

Okay, I _____ of the car – I _____ the underground. I'll call when I get there.

18.40 I'm out of the underground - there's a train broken down in the tunnel. I _____ to the bus stop round the corner.

AAAAAAAAH! _____ a hole in the pavement.

18.51 Okay, I'm off the bus. How long have I got?

Nine minutes

18.53 I _____ through the crowds. Now I'm on the bridge. I _____ breath.

18.59 Here I am at the theatre. Where are you?

18.42 I've climbed out of the hole. Oh! There's a bus. I _____

18.45 We _____ Charing Cross Road. Oh no! there's a demonstration. We can't get through.

Right behind you. You made it. Well done!

19.00 The tickets ... ah ... I thought you had the tickets ...

Where's Your Homework?

Make sentences to go with these excuses. Use the table to help you.

My father	ate	with it.
The queen	exploded.	
An eagle	stole	and took it back to his university.
My brother	came	my school bag.
My computer	landed in our garden	with it.
Some boys	took my homework	it.
A professor	made a paper plane	to tea.
The dog	lit the fire	and took my homework back to their planet.
Aliens	thought it was brilliant	and used it to make a nest

1 _The dog ate it._

2 _____

3 _____

4 _____

5 _____

6 _____

7 _____

8 _____

9 _____

Now, think of your own excuse and write it here.

10 _Actually,_ _____

Scary Stories

1 Put the verbs in the spaces.

2 Draw lines with three different colours to make three stories.

> **lived   landed**

Aliens _____ on the earth.

A family _____ on a windy hill.

> **heard   broke   went   sat**

A group of ten adults and
four children

_____ to the island of
Tunamo in the Pacific Ocean.

A boy with a hamburger
_____ their voices.

One night a bird _____
outside the window and _____
the glass.

> **lived   started   shouted   were**

The next night there _____
hundreds of birds.

Nobody _____ there and
they _____ a new society.

'Where are you?' he _____ .

> **couldn't   Help   lived**

'We are here. We are friendly.
_____ us,' they answered.

Only giant spiders _____
on the island.

The family _____ get out.

> **were   ate   caught**

He _____ his hamburger.

The birds _____ everywhere.

The spiders _____ eight
adults and four children in their
web.

> **escaped   was   killed**

The others _____ .

They _____ the family.

There _____ a loud crunch
in his mouth.

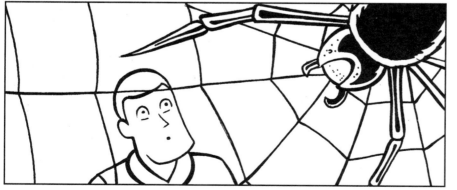

Now answer these questions.

1. Who killed the aliens? _____

2. Who did the spiders kill? _____

3. How many people escaped from Tunamo? _____

4. Who killed the family on the windy hill? _____

Michael Johnson - his feet never touch the ground

Read about Michael Johnson. Put the verbs into the past simple and fit them in the passage about him. Then, complete the grid with the verbs to find the answer to this question: What subject did Michael study at college?

He won 5 Olympic gold medals.

He (1) b roke_____ 6 world records.

He ran 200 metres in 19.32 seconds and 400 metres in 43.18 seconds.

He was born in Texas and he has lived all his life there. His dad (2) w_____ a truck driver. Everybody at school was amazed by his running talent. His high school coach said that his feet never (3) s_____ to touch the ground.

He went to college and (4) s_____ for a degree. While he was at college, he (5) r_____ that he could make a career in athletics. He was world no.1 at 200m and 400m by the age of 23. At the 1996 Atlanta Olympics, Johnson was the first athlete ever to win both the 200m and the 400m finals. The 200m final was his favourite race. 'That was as close as I've ever got to the perfect race,' he (6) s_____.

He soon became one of the highest paid athletes of all time. In 1997 he (7) s_____ a 6-year deal with Nike worth $12million. He was wearing special shoes when he (8) w_____ the 400m final at the Sydney Olympics in 2000 – they had pieces of real gold sewn into them.

He (9) r_____ in 2001 at the age of 33 when he was still at the top.

say
be
realise
seem
study
break
retire
sign
win

3) **S**

2) **W**

9) **R**

1) **B** R O K E

5) **R**

4) **S**

6) **S**

8) **W**

7) **S**

That's History!

Look at the timeline and answer the questions.

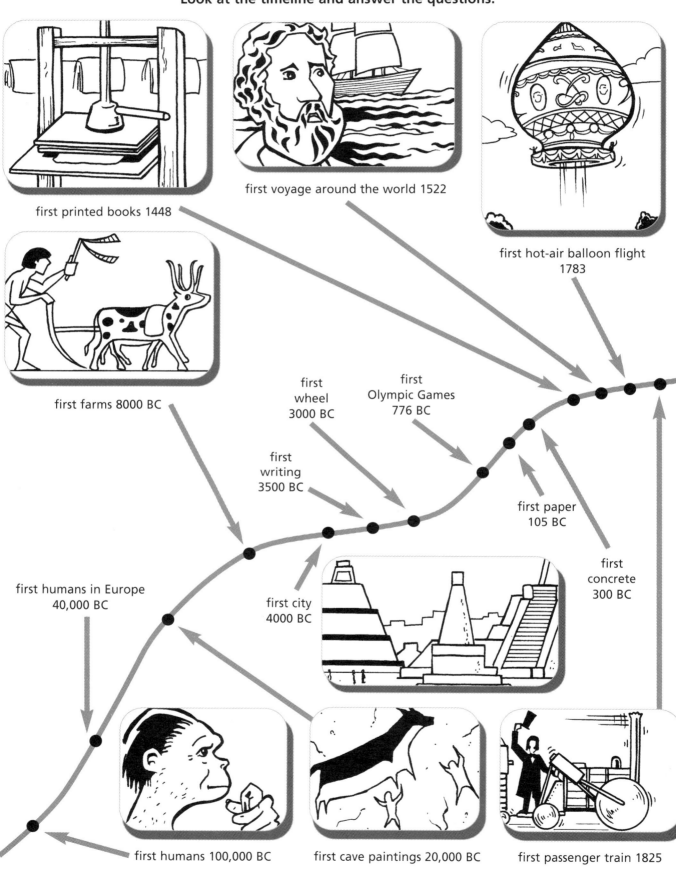

first printed books 1448

first voyage around the world 1522

first hot-air balloon flight 1783

first farms 8000 BC

first wheel 3000 BC

first Olympic Games 776 BC

first writing 3500 BC

first paper 105 BC

first concrete 300 BC

first humans in Europe 40,000 BC

first city 4000 BC

first humans 100,000 BC

first cave paintings 20,000 BC

first passenger train 1825

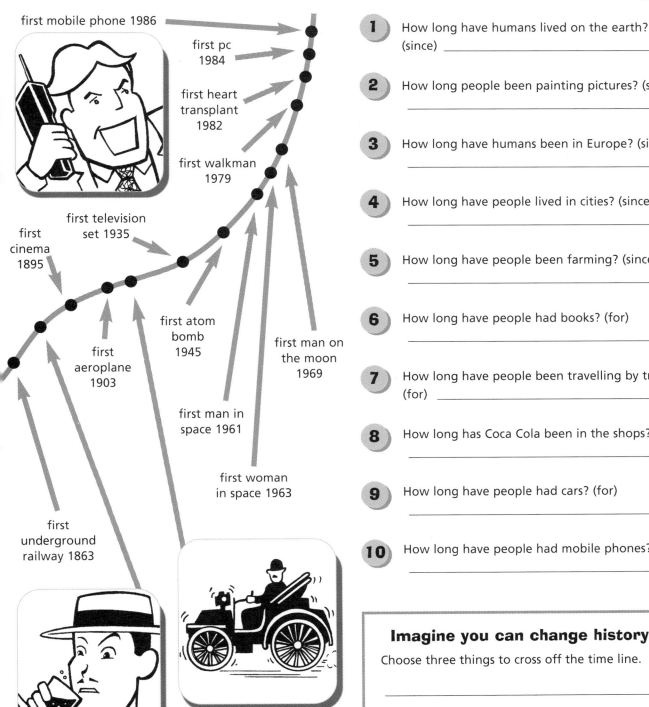

first mobile phone 1986

first pc
1984

first heart
transplant
1982

first walkman
1979

first television
set 1935

first
cinema
1895

first atom
bomb
1945

first man on
the moon
1969

first
aeroplane
1903

first man in
space 1961

first woman
in space 1963

first
underground
railway 1863

first car 1908

first glass of Coca Cola
drunk 1886

Add these things to the timeline

1 How long have humans lived on the earth?
(since) _____

2 How long people been painting pictures? (since)
_____

3 How long have humans been in Europe? (since)
_____

4 How long have people lived in cities? (since)
_____

5 How long have people been farming? (since)
_____

6 How long have people had books? (for)
_____

7 How long have people been travelling by train?
(for) _____

8 How long has Coca Cola been in the shops? (for)
_____

9 How long have people had cars? (for)
_____

10 How long have people had mobile phones? (for)
_____

Imagine you can change history.

Choose three things to cross off the time line.

_____

_____

_____

Think of three things to add to the time line.

_____

_____

_____

Changing Rooms

STUDENT A

You and your partner decide to give your best friend's room a new style.

1 This is your best friend's room.

2 Draw your changes here. Don't show your partner.

You can: move the furniture; change the flooring; paint or wallpaper the walls; decorate the blind; buy 3 new things. When you've finished, answer your partner's questions.

3 Find out what your partner has done to the room. Draw his/her changes here.

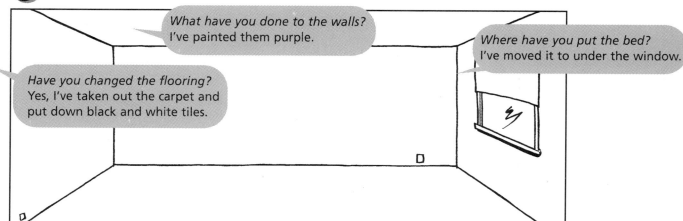

What have you done to the walls?
I've painted them purple.

Where have you put the bed?
I've moved it to under the window.

Have you changed the flooring?
Yes, I've taken out the carpet and put down black and white tiles.

Now compare your drawings with your partner's. They should be the same. Are they?

Changing Rooms

STUDENT B

You and your partner decide to give your best friend's room a new style.

1 This is your best friend's room.

2 Draw your changes here. Don't show your partner.

You can: move the furniture; change the flooring; paint or wallpaper the walls; decorate the blind; buy 3 new things. When you've finished, answer your partner's questions.

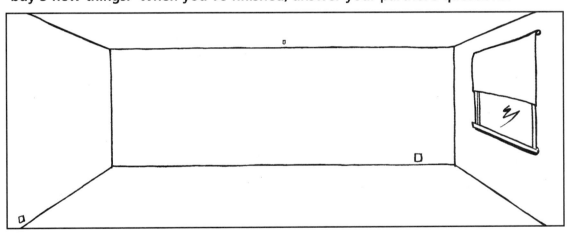

3 Find out what your partner has done to the room. Draw his/her changes here.

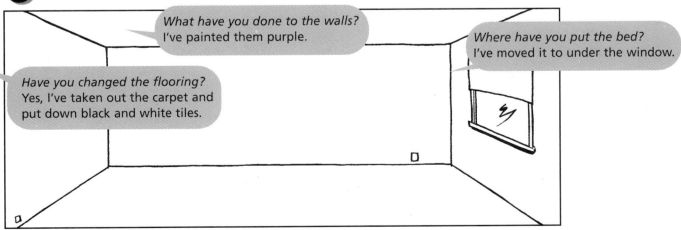

Now compare your drawings with your partner's. They should be the same. Are they?

Here is Today's News

News readers on radio and television often use the present perfect to tell the day's news stories.
These stories have got mixed up. First, sort out the sentences to make 8 possible stories.
Then, match the sentences to the pictures.

 ☐

 ☐

 ☐

 ☐

 ☐

 If

 ☐

 ☐

1 The government [f]

2 Three dangerous crocodiles ☐

3 A magician ☐

4 A restaurant chef ☐

5 Two schoolboys ☐

6 Detectives ☐

7 A vulture ☐

8 A pet rat ☐

a have climbed to the top of the Millennium Wheel.

b has saved his owners from a fire in their home.

c have arrested two monkeys for stealing cameras at the zoo.

d has crashed into an aeroplane at a height of 10,000 metres.

e have escaped from the aquarium.

f has introduced a new tax on chocolate.

g has attacked his customers with a kitchen knife.

h has lost his wife in a magic box.

Work with a partner. Choose one of the headlines. Invent the details of the rest of the story.

Pompeii

Read the text. Then, answer the questions.

Today is August 24, AD 79. We are in Pompeii, a small town in southern Italy, during the time of the Roman Empire. The town lies just below Mount Vesuvius, an ancient volcano. Farmers grow food on the slopes of the mountain.

People are busy in the town. Let's walk down the main street. First we pass a taverna. A young man is drinking a glass of wine at the bar. Next we smell fresh bread from the bakery. Two women are buying loaves and honey cakes. In the road a crowd of children are playing a game with stones. Maximus Minimus walks past – he lives behind the bakery. He invites us in. We follow him into his open air courtyard. His wife, Agrippina, is here, writing a letter. The workmen are painting pictures of the countryside on the walls. A dog is sleeping in the corner.

Suddenly there is an explosion. The sky goes dark. The ground shakes violently. There is lightning. Everybody thinks it is an earthquake, but they are wrong. It is the volcano. After 800 years, Mount Vesuvius has woken up. Fire and lava burst out of the top. Black clouds of hot ash fill the sky and the wind takes them over Pompeii. Maximus grabs Agrippina's hand and they run out of the house. The dog hides under a table. The children cry for their parents. Men, women, children and animals run through the streets. Most of them escape but two thousand die.

When it is over, the sky stays dark. Piles of ash cover everything. It looks like snow.

1 What was the young man doing when the volcano erupted?

_____

2 What were the two women doing?

_____

3 What were the children doing?

_____

4 What was Agrippina doing?

_____

5 What were the workmen doing?

_____

6 What was the dog doing?

_____

7 What did Maximus do when the volcano erupted?

_____

8 What did the dog do?

_____

9 What did the children do?

_____

10 What happened to the people of Pompeii?

_____

Memory Test

Look at this page for 1 minute.

YESTERDAY EVENING 8.30

Mark   *Lulu*   *Julia and Marlon*

THIS MORNING 11.00

THIS AFTERNOON 4.00

Now, cover this page and answer the questions that your teacher gave you.

Memory Test

What can you remember?

1 What was Lulu doing at 11.00 this morning? _____

2 What was Mark doing at 8.30 yesterday evening? _____

3 What were Julia and Marlon doing at 8.30 yesterday evening? _____

4 When was Lulu flying a helicopter? _____

5 When were Julia and Marlon playing their guitars? _____

6 What was Lulu doing at 4.00 this afternoon? _____

7 What was Mark doing at 11.00 this morning? _____

8 When was Mark ice-skating? _____

9 What was Mark doing at 11.00 this morning? _____

10 What was Mark doing at 4.00 this afternoon? _____

How many did you remember?

What were <u>you</u> doing at:

8.30 yesterday evening?

_____

11.00 this morning?

_____

4.00 this afternoon?

_____

Talk to a partner. Ask him/her what he/she was doing at different times yesterday. Keep asking until you find a time when you were both doing the same thing.

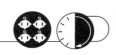

A Fishy Story

Read the story and put the pictures in the order that they actually happened.

One strange day, fish fell out of the sky. It happened like this. I had gone to the shops to buy vegetables for supper and a bone for my dog. It wasn't raining when I left but I had taken my umbrella anyway. I got to the shops and bought the things I wanted. I was walking home when suddenly there was a loud bang and the sky went very dark. I looked up to see black shapes falling towards me. In an instant the shapes began to hit the ground. They hit me, too and knocked me over. They were fish. I was amazed. I looked around. Other people had come out into the street when they heard the noise. Nobody could explain it. That evening our street was on television. An old bomb from the war had exploded in the river that runs through the town. The bomb had lain at the bottom of the river for fifty years. So that night we had fish for supper with our vegetables.

Amazon Diary

Ben was on an expedition through the Amazon when he lost the other people in his group. Here's part of his diary. Cut out the blocks of letters below and stick them in the correct spaces to complete the story.

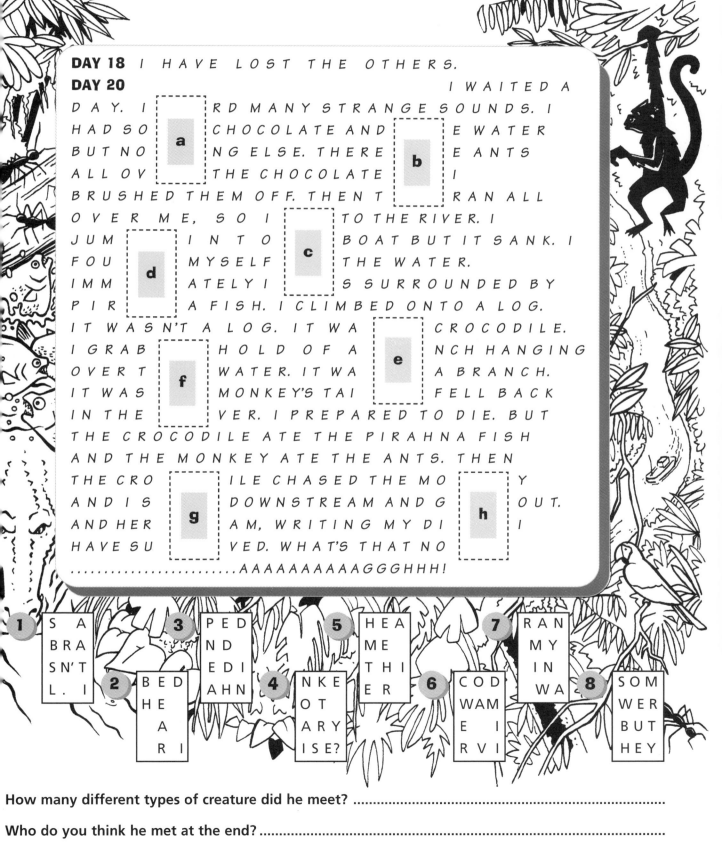

DAY 18 I HAVE LOST THE OTHERS.
DAY 20 I WAITED A
DAY. I [a] RD MANY STRANGE SOUNDS. I
HAD SO [a] CHOCOLATE AND [b] E WATER
BUT NO [a] NG ELSE. THERE [b] E ANTS
ALL OV [a] THE CHOCOLATE [b] I
BRUSHED THEM OFF. THEN T [b] RAN ALL
OVER ME, SO I [c] TO THE RIVER. I
JUM [d] IN TO [c] BOAT BUT IT SANK. I
FOU [d] MYSELF [c] THE WATER.
IMM [d] ATELY I [c] S SURROUNDED BY
PIR [d] A FISH. I CLIMBED ONTO A LOG.
IT WASN'T A LOG. IT WA [e] CROCODILE.
I GRAB [f] HOLD OF A [e] NCH HANGING
OVER T [f] WATER. IT WA [e] A BRANCH.
IT WAS [f] MONKEY'S TAI [e] FELL BACK
IN THE [f] VER. I PREPARED TO DIE. BUT
THE CROCODILE ATE THE PIRAHNA FISH
AND THE MONKEY ATE THE ANTS. THEN
THE CRO [g] ILE CHASED THE MO [h] Y
AND I S [g] DOWNSTREAM AND G [h] OUT.
AND HER [g] AM, WRITING MY DI [h] I
HAVE SU [g] VED. WHAT'S THAT NO [h]
.......................AAAAAAAAAAGGGHHH!

1
S A
BRA
SN'T
L. I

2
BED
HE
A
RI

3
P E D
N D
E D I
A H N

4
N K E
O T
A R Y
I S E?

5
H E A
M E
T H I
E R

6
C O D
W A M
E I
R V I

7
R A N
M Y
I N
W A

8
S O M
W E R
B U T
H E Y

How many different types of creature did he meet? ....

Who do you think he met at the end? ....

Trip to Town

You're going to town.

The time now is 9.50am. Your mum gives you this list.

return books
pay cheque into
*   account*
new trainers
haircut
buy: shampoo
*   toothpaste*
*   large loaf*
*   cakes for tea*
buy stamps and
*   post parcel*

This is your list:

new CD
hire video for this
*   evening*
meet friends at
burger bar 12.15

Add your own ideas:

....
....
....

This is what your mum says to you as you're going out of the door:

Remember the bank shuts at 12.00.

Don't forget the bakery sells out early.

Your hair appointment is at 11.30 - it'll take about half an hour.

Don't miss the 11 o'clock post.

Hurry up! You'll miss the bus. It leaves in 10 minutes.

BUS TIMETABLE
leaves	9.30	10.00	11.30
arrives	10.00	10.30	12.00

MUSIC / VIDEO MEGASTORE

LIBRARY
Opening hours
Mon-Sat 9.30-4.00

CYBER CAFE

The Bread Basket

cool shoes

The Hair Shop

Boots *the chemist*

POST OFFICE
Open Mon-Sat
9.00am - 5.30pm

Trip to Town

On the bus you plan what you are going to do, using all the information on these pages.

Like this:

10.30 *bank*

11.30 *hair cut ...*

Then a friend gets on the bus. The time now is 10.15. He/She asks you what you're going to do today. Tell him/her, like this:

First, I'm going to the bank. Then, ...

Use words like these:

First, Next, Then, After that, Last

Compare your plan with another student's. If there are differences, explain your plan, like this:

I'm going to the bakery first because they sell out early.

_____

_____

_____

_____

_____

_____

What is Going to Happen Next?

Make 8 predictions like this: *The little boy is going to fall into the hole.*

1. The ants _____
2. The crocodile _____
3. The bridge _____
4. The swing _____
5. The bull _____
6. The monkey _____
7. The newspaper _____
8. The little dog _____

Vote for Us

① We will – reduce crime

② We will – help farmers

③ We will – protect the countryside

④ We will – prepare our young people for the future

⑤ We will – build new, cheap houses

⑥ We will – modernise our transport system

⑦ We will – create more jobs

FIVE YEARS LATER...

1. No _____
2. _____
3. _____
4. _____
5. _____
6. _____
7. _____
8. _____
9. _____
10. _____

Have the Forward Party's predictions come true? Read these newspaper stories and write yes or no in the spaces above.

STREET CRIME UP   There were 40% more street crimes in the last three months.

NUMBERS OF WILD ANIMALS INCREASE
There are more hedgehogs, foxes, wild rabbits and badgers in our countryside than ever before.

'WHERE ARE OUR COMPUTERS?'
School teachers complained to the government yesterday that they had no computers in their classrooms.

MORE JOBS   The number of employed people rose again last month.

FARM PROTEST
Hundreds of farmers drove their tractors around Parliament Square yesterday to protest against falling milk prices.

HOMES FOR THE POOR   New houses for people on low incomes are now available.

TRAFFIC ISN'T MOVING
Drivers in Southampton city centre were angry yesterday when roadworks on the main roads caused hours of delay.

On Tour

STUDENT A

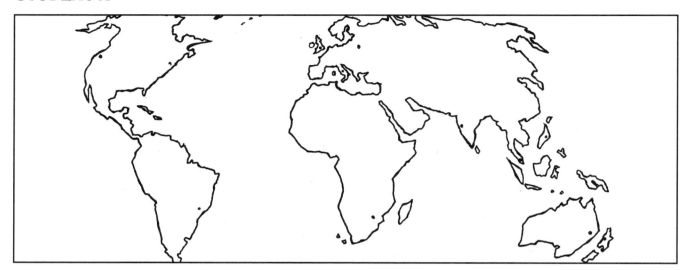

You and Student B are members of a new pop group. You come from New Zealand and you are going on a tour around the world to promote your band, staying in some cities only long enough to give an interview or do a concert. You have half the itinerary. Student B has the other half. Don't show each other your information. Talk about your plans like this:

Where do we fly to from Tokyo?

We fly to Moscow. Then we stay the night there.

Mark on the map where you spend each night with this symbol .

Sometimes you spend the night in the air.

Neither of you knows where you are spending the final night. Wait until the end to find out.

ITINERARY

Day 1 Monday
Leave Auckland midnight. Arrive Vancouver, Canada, the following morning. Lunchtime TV interview. Perform at pop festival in the afternoon. Leave Vancouver 8pm.

Day 3 Wednesday
Arrive Sao Paulo at 2pm. Breakfast with clients. Appear on TV and perform. Hotel in Sao Paulo Wednesday night. Fly out 8am.

Day 5 Friday
Appear in breakfast TV. Fly to London at 12 noon. 12 hour flight. 2 hour time difference. Central London hotel.

Day 7 Sunday morning. Arrive Bombay. Day off. Sightseeing. Relaxing. Evening – do concert.

Day 9 Tuesday. Morning meeting. Fly to Tokyo. Evening concert. Fly out.

What is the name of your band?

Take the third letter of the fourth city you visited, the second letter of the second city you visited, the last letter of the first city you visited and the fourth letter of the sixth city you went to.

Now, take the first letter of the city that you visited on day nine, the second letter of the fifth city you visited, the last letter of the city you live in, the second letter of the third city and the last letter of the city you visited on day eight.

Write the letters on the poster.

ARE COMING TO YOUR TOWN SOON!

On Tour

STUDENT B

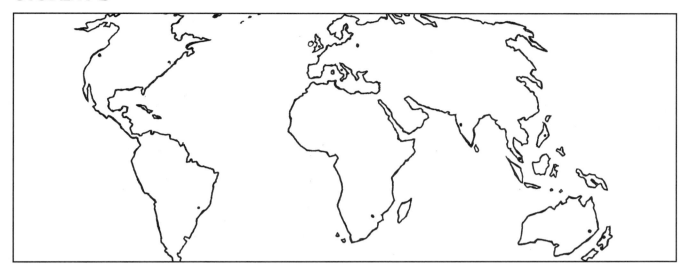

You and Student B are members of a new pop group. You come from New Zealand and you are going on a tour around the world to promote your band, staying in some cities only long enough to give an interview or do a concert. You have half the itinerary. Student B has the other half. Don't show each other your information. Talk about your plans like this:

> *Where do we fly to from Tokyo?*

> We fly to Moscow. Then we stay the night there.

Mark on the map where you spend each night with this symbol .

Sometimes you spend the night in the air.

Neither of you knows where you are spending the final night. Wait until the end to find out.

ITINERARY

Day 2 Tuesday
Arrive New York early morning. Lunch and then interviews with magazine journalists in the afternoon. Do concert at 7pm. Leave New York at 12 midnight.

Day 4 Thursday
Arrive Johannesburg 10pm local time. Hotel.

Day 6 Saturday
Appear on breakfast TV. Fly to Rome. Lunchtime interview. Fly to Moscow. Evening concert. Fly out overnight.

Day 8 Monday
Lie-in in Bombay. Fly out in the afternoon. Arrive Singapore mid-evening. Evening concert.

Day 10 Wednesday morning. Arrive Sydney. Morning interview. Then fly back to Auckland.

What is the name of your band?

Take the third letter of the fourth city you visited, the second letter of the second city you visited, the last letter of the first city you visited and the fourth letter of the sixth city you went to.

Now, take the first letter of the city that you visited on day nine, the second letter of the fifth city you visited, the last letter of the city you live in, the second letter of the third city and the last letter of the city you visited on day eight.

Write the letters on the poster.

ARE COMING TO YOUR TOWN SOON!

Diary Battleships

1 Find a partner. You are Student A and your partner is Student B.

2 Below you will see a copy of your diary. DO NOT SHOW IT TO STUDENT B.

3 You and Student B are brother and sister. It's the first week of the holidays and your mother wants you to help her with the housework. You and Student B both have three free periods during the first week of the holidays. You must find all 3 of Student B's free periods by asking him/her questions e.g. *What are you doing on Friday morning? What are you doing on Tuesday evening?* Take it in turns – Student A asks a question, then, Student B asks a question. You are the winner if you find all of Student B's free periods before he/she finds yours.

4 The loser has to help your mother with the housework!

STUDENT A

	FRI	SAT	SUN	MON	TUES	WED	THURS
morning	free	working at the shoe shop	visiting grandma	going to choir practice	going to the dentist	going to choir practice	babysitting my little brother for my parents
afternoon	shopping for Joe's birthday present	working at the shoe shop		free	going shopping with Mum	taking the cat to the vet	
evening	going to Joe's birthday party	travelling to visit grandma	travelling home	cooking dinner for my family	free	going ice-skating with Laura	singing in concert

Write Student B's answers here.

	FRI	SAT	SUN	MON	TUES	WED	THURS
morning							
afternoon							
evening							

Diary Battleships

1 Find a partner. You are Student B and your partner is Student A.

2 Below you will see a copy of your diary. DO NOT SHOW IT TO STUDENT A.

3 You and Student A are brother and sister. It's the first week of the holidays and your mother wants you to help her with the housework. You and Student A both have three free periods during the first week of the holidays. You must find all 3 of Student A's free periods by asking him/her questions e.g. *What are you doing on Friday morning? What are you doing on Tuesday evening?* Take it in turns – Student A asks a question, then, Student B asks a question. You are the winner if you find all of Student B's free periods before he/she finds yours.

4 The loser has to help your mother with the housework!

STUDENT B

	FRI	SAT	SUN	MON	TUES	WED	THURS
morning	going for holiday job interview	going shopping	helping to prepare the village fete	going swimming	going	going horse-riding	free
afternoon	going to basketball practice	free	going to village fete	doing piano practice	on	babysitting for my neighbour	having my hair cut
evening	going to piano lesson	baking cakes for the village fete	going to the cinema with Mike	playing in basketball match	day out	free	working on my holiday project with my study partner

Write Student A's answers here.

	FRI	SAT	SUN	MON	TUES	WED	THURS
morning							
afternoon							
evening							

Emergency!

Do you know what to do in a crisis? Choose the correct answer.
Your teacher will tell you how many points you get at the end.

1 **If your friend has a nosebleed,**
(a) you tell him to sit down and put his head between his knees.
(b) you tell him to stand on his head and drink a glass of water.
(c) you suddenly shout very loudly in his ear.

2 **If the fire alarm goes off at school,**
(a) you walk through the building and look for smoke and flames.
(b) you go outside and call the fire brigade.
(c) you don't do anything – it goes off all the time.

3 **If a chemical spills in the science classroom at school,**
(a) you wipe it up with a cloth.
(b) you find a teacher at once.
(c) you leave it – it will soon dry.

4 **If you see a dog in the street with no owner and no collar,**
(a) you catch it and stroke it.
(b) you don't do anything.
(c) you report it to the Council.

5 **If you come home and smell gas,**
(a) you switch the light on and check the house.
(b) you close the door and call the gas company from your neighbours' house.
(c) you don't worry about it.

6 **If there is a fire in the kitchen,**
(a) you stay in the room and open the windows.
(b) you go out of the room, close the door, out of the house and call the fire brigade.
(c) you open all the doors in the house.

7 **If you knock a tooth out in a football game,**
(a) you wrap it up in a tissue and take it home.
(b) you put it under your tongue and go to your dentist.
(c) you put it in a glass of milk and go to your dentist.

8 **If you cut your arm and it bleeds a lot,**
(a) you hold your arm up in the air.
(b) you sit down and hold your arm up in the air.
(c) you lie down with your arm by your side.

9 **If you find a burglar in your house,**
(a) you try to catch him.
(b) you run out of the house and call for help.
(c) you offer him a cup of tea.

10 **If you get hiccups,**
(a) you put your head in a bucket.
(b) you stand on your head and drink a glass of water.
(c) you wait until they go.

April Fool

**It's April 1st. Mr Jones, the English teacher, has left the classroom for a few minutes.
His naughty students have decided to play some April Fool's tricks on him.
Look at the picture and then fill in the missing words in the sentences below.**

1   If h e   opens t he   door, t he   flour w   fall o   his h .

2   I   he l   in h   desk, a f   will j   out.

3   If h   sits d , he w   stick t   his c .

4   I   he w   on t   board, t   pen w   rub o .

5   If h   plays t   cassette, h   will h   pop m .

6   I   he o   his b , he w   find a squashed t .

7   If h   drinks h   coffee, i   will t   disgusting!

What a Change!

Watch this stone change into a tortoise.

> If this stone *came alive*, it would walk *like* a tortoise.

What will these objects change into? Draw lines to join the objects to the animals they become.

Take words from these boxes to make sentences. Use your dictionary if you're not sure what they mean.

If this stapler �_____ alive, it _____ a dog.

stapler	**teapot**
hair clip	**mouse**
pencil	**toy car**

look
move
walk
run

snake	**beetle**
dog	**spider**
monkey	**elephant**

Morph your own object.
Draw an object.   Draw the creature it turns into.

Choose from:

Show it to your partner. He/She makes a sentence about it.

What Kind of Artist Are You?

We're all artistic, but we express ourselves in different ways.
Do you express yourself best in pictures, music, words or with your body?
First of all, fill in the gaps using the words in brackets to make second conditional sentences.
Then, answer the questions and find out.

1 If you _____ (have) half an hour to spare now, what _____ (do)?

(a) read a book
(b) draw a picture
(c) listen to some music
(d) go outside and play football

2 If you _____ (go) to the theatre this evening, what _____ (choose) to see?

(a) a ballet
(b) a modern play
(c) a Shakespeare play
(d) a musical

3 If you _____ (go) to see your favourite band this evening, what _____ (do) in the half hour before you went?

(a) worry about your clothes
(b) listen to the band's CD
(c) practise your dancing
(d) find out facts about the band

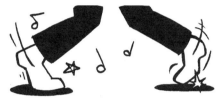

4 If your English teacher _____ (ask) you to choose a fun class activity, which one _____ (choose)?

(a) playing a game
(b) watching a TV programme or film
(c) listening to a song
(d) discussion

5 If these teachers _____ (met) your parents, who _____ (say) the nicest things about you?

(a) your art teacher
(b) your music teacher
(c) your language teacher
(d) your sports teacher

6 Heroes....

If you _____ (choose) one person to represent America, who _____ (choose)?

(a) Michael Jordan
(b) Madonna
(c) Ernest Hemingway
(d) Andy Warhol

- -

19-24 You are a words person - you read about a painting before you look at it, you read about music before you listen to it.

13-18 You are a visual person - you always look first and find out information later.

7-12 Music comes first for you - you are happiest when you are playing or listening to music.

0-6 You express yourself with your body - you like to do things yourself rather than watch other people do them.

SCORES: 1a-4 1b-3 1c-2 1d-1; 2a-1 2b-3 2c-4 2d-2; 3a-3 3b-2 3c-1 3d-4; 4a-1 4b-3 4c-2 4d-4; 5a-3 5b-2 5c-4 5d-1; 6a-1 6b-2 6c-4 6d-3.

A Tropical Island is Born

These pictures show how a tropical island is born. Before you read the text below,
try to put the pictures in order. Can you say what is happening in the pictures?
Use the present passive if you can.

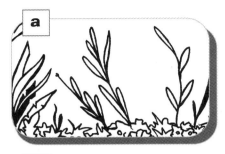

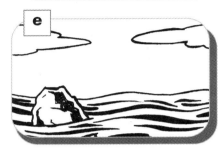

Look these words up in your dictionary:

> coral   limestone   dust   germinate   decay   layer   ecosystem

Choose a verb for each space and put it into the present passive.

> blow   create   cover   break down   replace   trap   build up

Coral builds up over time in warm waters and eventually it breaks through the surface of the sea. At first nothing
can live on it - it is bare rock. Over time the coral limestone _____ by the wind, rain and sea. The
limestone becomes dust and _____ in cracks in the rock. Seeds _____ across the new
island by the wind. Some land in the cracks where they germinate and grow. They flower, turn to seed, die and
then decay. Slowly a layer of organic material _____ on the island. Other plants now grow and
eventually a complete ecosystem _____ . Gradually small plants _____ by taller
plants. Eventually the island _____ in trees - unless humans arrive and cut them down.

Did you put your pictures in the right order?

What's It Made Of?

Use the words in the box to complete the sentences. Write the words in the puzzle.
Find out what Jen's dress is made of.

> glass   metal   rubber   stone   rope   brick   paper   plastic   ice   wool

1 Books are made of _____ .

2 The Eiffel Tower is made of _____ .

3 These toys are made of _____ .

4 The pyramids are made of _____ .

5 These tyres are made of _____ .

6 Icebergs are made of _____ .

7 This jumper is made of _____ .

8 This wall is made of _____ .

9 This swing is made of _____ .

10 This bottle is made of _____ .

What's your skirt made of, Jen?

It's made of __ __ __ __ __ __ __ __

What's Happened to You?

What have these people had/got done? Complete the speech bubbles.
Find the past participles you need in the wordsearch.

1 I've __had__ my __hair__ __cut__

I've _____ my _____ _____

I	P	I	E	R	C	E	D
T	A	V	E	H	U	A	M
E	I	D	M	Y	T	P	E
S	N	H	O	T	T	O	N
T	T	G	R	A	A	P	D
E	E	H	T	K	A	K	E
D	D	D	Y	E	D	E	D
C	L	E	A	N	E	D	N

2

3 I've _____ my _____ _____

4 I've_____ my _____ _____ _____

5 I've_____ my _____ _____ out!

6 We've_____ our _____ _____

7 I've_____ my _____ _____

WTI
YAKB
D C L S N
N O J X

8 I've_____ my _____ _____

Write the leftover letters from the wordsearch above to complete
the sentence. Draw a picture to go with the sentence.

_ _ _ ' _
_ _ _ _ _

Great Natural Disasters

Put the pictures in order. Put the missing verbs in the captions in the past simple passive.
Choose the verbs from the box.

hit   bury   melt   burn   drown

A

under a mountain
of ash. [3]

When Mt Vesuvius
erupted in AD79,

the Roman town
of Pompeii _____

B
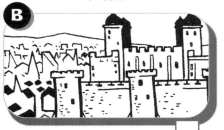

the city of
London

_____
to the ground.

PUDDING LANE

A fire started in Pudding
Lane in London in 1666 and

C

When the Titanic
hit an iceberg in 1912,

over 1,500 people
_____

in the icy waters of
the Atlantic Ocean.

D

the iron skyscrapers
_____

to the ground by the
heat.

In the Great Fire
of 1871 in Chicago,

E

by 15-metre-high
waves.

After a terrible
earthquake in Portugal in 1775,

the city of Lisbon
_____

Zak's Coffee Bar

Zak has a new girl working for him on Saturdays. He shows her the list of rules.
Write *must* or *mustn't* in the gaps.

RULES

1. You _____ always smile at the customers.
2. You _____ ever be rude.
3. There _____ be a queue of more than five customers.
4. The tables _____ always be cleaned before a new customer sits down.
5. Customers _____ smoke in the non-smoking areas.
6. You _____ sweep the floor every half hour.
7. You _____ eat or drink while you are working.
8. You _____ ask people who don't buy anything to leave.
9. Coffee and tea _____ always be served really hot.
10. Long hair _____ be tied back.

Here's the cafe at lunchtime. Which rules are being broken?

Write the numbers in the boxes. ☐ ☐ ☐ ☐ ☐

Can you think of any more rules that Zak could put on his list? Write them here.

_____

Class Survey

1 Work in a small group. Decide which of your classmates' names to write as the answer for each question.

2 Now ask the students whose names you wrote. Are your answers correct?
Example: Oscar, can you windsurf?
If the answer is "No", ask another student. Find a name for each question.

3 When you have found a student who answers "Yes", find out when they were first able to do this. Ask "When could you first do this?".

Find someone who...	NAME	When could he/she first do this?
1 can windsurf.	_____	_____
2 can speak 2 foreign languages.	_____	_____
3 can juggle.	_____	_____
4 can cook.	_____	_____
5 can read music.	_____	_____
6 can touch-type.	_____	_____
7 can ride a horse.	_____	_____
8 can sing well.	_____	_____
9 can play tennis well.	_____	_____
10 can look after a baby.	_____	_____

The Rainbow Cafe

Here's part of the menu.

SANDWICHES

beef	2.50
tuna and cucumber	2.00
cheese and tomato	1.25
smoked salmon and cream cheese	2.50

ROLLS

egg	1.00
egg and bacon	1.30
cheese and tomato	1.00
ham and salad	2.00

SOUPS

pea	2.00
tomato	2.00
beetroot	3.00

SALADS

red salad: tomatoes, red peppers, carrot, beetroot	4.25
green salad: cucumber, lettuce, spinach, herbs	3.75
yellow salad: cheese, sweetcorn, yellow pepper	4.50

DRINKS

orange juice	1.25
apple juice	1.25
carrot juice	1.25
coffee	1.00
tea	1.00
milk	.75

HOT MEALS

omelette	3.00
hamburger	3.50

with

chips	.50
broccoli	.50
carrots	.50
baked beans	.50

1 Fill in the gaps with forms of *would* (*'d*) and *like*.

TABLE 1

I'd _____ omelette and broccoli. What _____ you _____?

I__ _____ a very healthy lunch - tomato soup and green salad.

TABLE 2

I think I__ _____ a bowl of pea soup and a carrot and beetroot salad. How about you?

Yes, that's right.

Is the soup vegetarian?

Okay. I__ _____ exactly the same as you.

TABLE 3

I'm having a beef sandwich. _____ you _____ one, too?

No, I _____, thanks. I'll have an egg and bacon roll. And we'll get two coffees, please.

TABLE 4

What shall we have? Well, I__ _____ orange juice and a hamburger. What _____ you _____?

I'll have an egg roll and a cheese salad.

2 Which table do these bills go to?

BILL 1	BILL 2	BILL 3	BILL 4
3.50	1.30	3.00	2.00 x2
1.25	2.50	.50	4.25 x2
4.50	1.00 x2	2.00	
1.00	_____	3.75	_____
_____	5.80	_____	12.50
10.25		11.25	

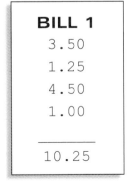 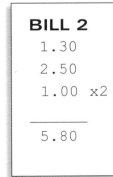 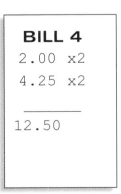

3 You are in the Rainbow Cafe with a friend. Order lunch. Help each other to choose, using *Would you like ...?* Work out how much your bill will be.

School's Out

We're free! What shall we do?
Each friend has a different suggestion about what to do. Can you decide which option makes a
correct grammatical sentence? Check your answer by following the line.
If you find the right picture, your answer is correct.

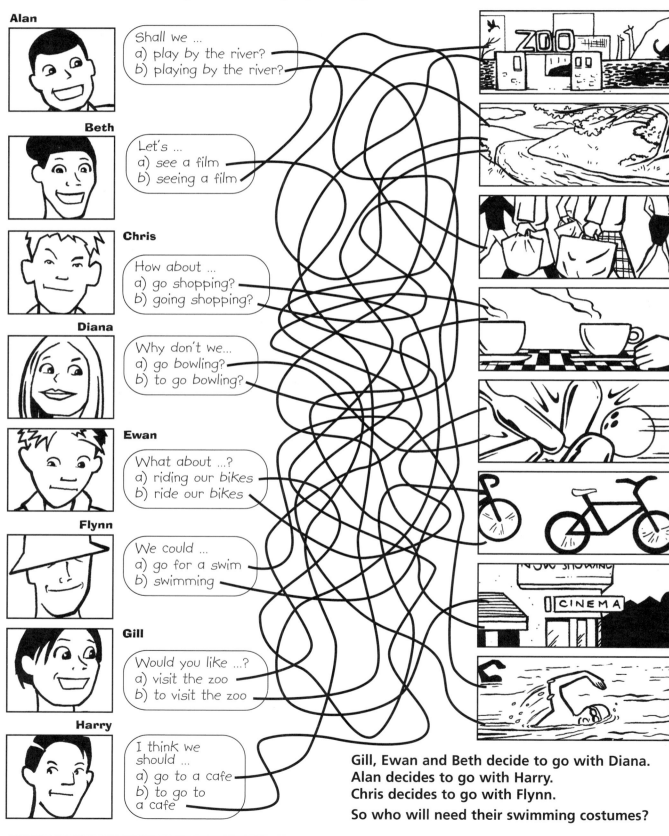

Alan

Shall we ...
a) play by the river?
b) playing by the river?

Beth

Let's ...
a) see a film
b) seeing a film

Chris

How about ...
a) go shopping?
b) going shopping?

Diana

Why don't we...
a) go bowling?
b) to go bowling?

Ewan

What about ...?
a) riding our bikes
b) ride our bikes

Flynn

We could ...
a) go for a swim
b) swimming

Gill

Would you like ...?
a) visit the zoo
b) to visit the zoo

Harry

I think we
should ...
a) go to a cafe
b) to go to
a cafe

Gill, Ewan and Beth decide to go with Diana.
Alan decides to go with Harry.
Chris decides to go with Flynn.

So who will need their swimming costumes?

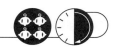

What Are You Allowed to Do?

Work in a group of four. Ask the other three students these questions and put their answers in the boxes. Put a tick (✔) for "Yes" and a cross (✗) for "No".
Read the analysis. Who has the easiest life?

Are you allowed to ...	Friend A	Friend B	Friend C	Me
stay in bed late at the weekend?				
go to the shops by yourself?				
have a pet?				
watch television after 10pm?				
go out on your bike by yourself?				
invite your friends to your house without asking your parents?				
stay at home by yourself?				
cook supper?				
have parties?				
have boyfriends/girlfriends?				
wear whatever clothes you want?				
have a mobile phone?				
eat sweets or snacks between meals?				
play loud music?				
put your feet on the furniture?				

ANALYSIS

Count how many ticks (✔) you have.

10 -14 (✔) You have an easy life. Your parents aren't strict at all and like you to make your own decisions. However, sometimes it can be harder to take responsibility and decide for yourself what you should do.

5 - 9 Your life is not easy but it's not hard either. Your parents have rules but they are probably fair and reasonable.

0 - 4 Your life is hard! Perhaps you like having plenty of rules to follow. If you show your parents how responsible you are, they may give you more freedom.

Now write about the results. Use phrases like these:
All of us ...
Three of us are allowed to ...
One of us ...
None of us is allowed to ...

1 _____

2 _____

3 _____

4 _____

5 _____

6 _____

Our Bodies

Find the right verb to complete these sentences. Write the numbers of the sentences in the correct place on the picture.

to breathe	to stand up	to write and draw	to pump
to chew	to see	to eat	to balance	to run	to store

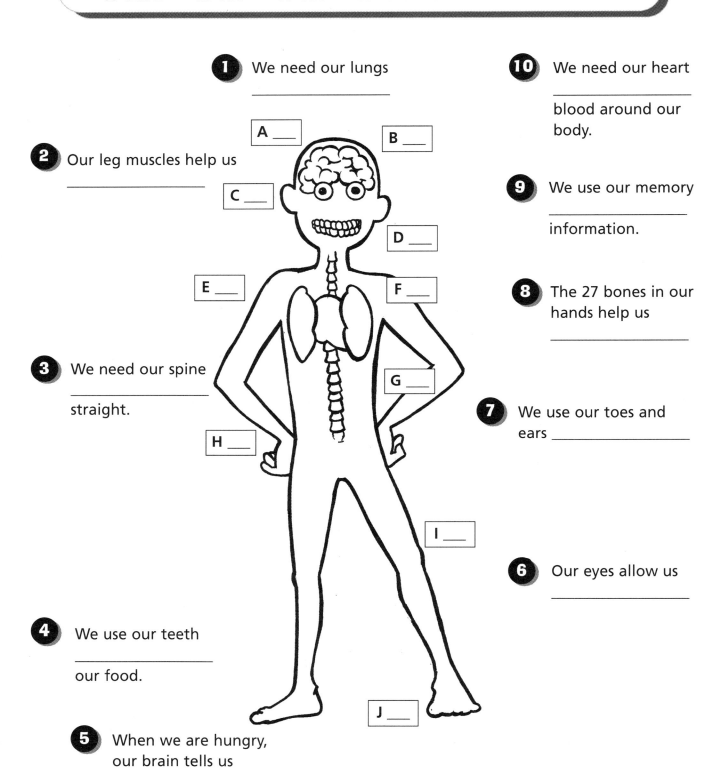

1 We need our lungs
_____

2 Our leg muscles help us
_____

3 We need our spine
_____
straight.

4 We use our teeth
_____
our food.

5 When we are hungry,
our brain tells us
_____

A ___   B ___   C ___   D ___   E ___   F ___   G ___   H ___   I ___   J ___

10 We need our heart
_____
blood around our
body.

9 We use our memory
_____
information.

8 The 27 bones in our
hands help us
_____

7 We use our toes and
ears _____

6 Our eyes allow us
_____

To: Ben@astro.co.uk

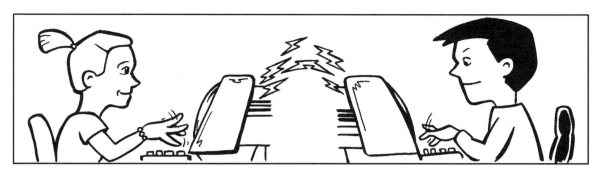

Ben and Jan are with their class in the computer room. Their teacher, Miss Jones, is there too.
Miss Jones thinks they are doing their homework. They're actually having an email conversation.

1 Write the question tags in the spaces.

2 Put the messages in the right order.

To:	Ben@astro.co.uk
Subject:	the beach

a. But suppose we see them on the beach. Then there'll be trouble,
(1)...........?

b. Sure, Ben. But you won't be able to come, (2).............?

c. We can't go to the beach this weekend, (3).............?

d. Mrs J thinks we're doing our homework, (4).............?

e. You're going to your cousins' house, (5).............?

SEND

To:	Jan@whistlejacket.co.uk
Subject:	Sea and sand

f. Well, perhaps I can come. I can tell my mum that you're ill in bed and I
have to visit you. Then we can go to the beach, (6)...........?

g. Why can't we?

h. No, Jan, she doesn't. She's standing right behind you.

i. I know. I'll say that you need the sea air because you're ill.

j. No, I'm not. They're coming to see us instead. Help! You can't invite me
to your house, (7)...........?

SEND

Work with a partner. Have an email conversation (either on screen or using pieces of paper).

Football Crazy!
STUDENT A

Look at your picture. Student B has the same picture but with ten differences. Take turns to ask questions to find the differences. Questions can only have Yes/No answers.

e.g. *Is the goalkeeper's shirt white?*   *Yes, it is./No, it isn't.*

Keep a record of how many questions you ask.

How many questions did you have to ask to find the differences?

Write your answer here ☐. Compare with another pair of students.

| You *might* need these words. |
| goalkeeper   referee   whistle |
| linesman   flag   net   pigeon |
| goalpost   advert   stadium |
| player   pitch |

Football Crazy!
STUDENT B

Look at your picture. Student A has the same picture but with ten differences. Take turns to ask questions to find the differences. Questions can only have Yes/No answers.

e.g. *Is the goalkeeper's shirt striped?   Yes, it is./No, it isn't.*

Keep a record of how many questions you ask.

How many questions did you have to ask to find the differences?

Write your answer here ☐. Compare with another pair of students.

> **You *might* need these words.**
>
> goalkeeper   referee   whistle
>
> linesman   flag   net   pigeon
>
> goalpost   advert   stadium
>
> player   pitch

Fortune Teller

Cut out the square of paper on the other page.

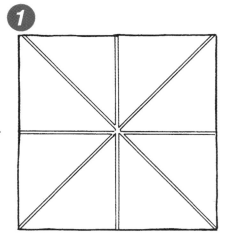

- Fold all the corners D, E, F, G into the middle point C.

- Turn this over and fold all those corners into the middle point **1**.

- Fold this in half **2**.

- Put one thumb and one finger of each hand in the four paper pockets **3**.

- Draw four different colour circles, one on the outside of each pocket **4**.

- Open the fortune teller. Write numbers 1 - 8 on the eight small triangles inside **5**.

- Open each big triangle **6**. Write these fortunes:

  You will marry many times.
  You will become a great professor.
  You will have lots of children.
  You will be famous.
  You will be powerful.
  You will travel to amazing places.
  You will live a quiet life.
  You will have a lot of money.

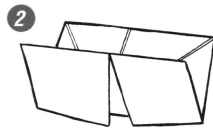

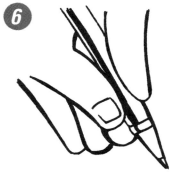

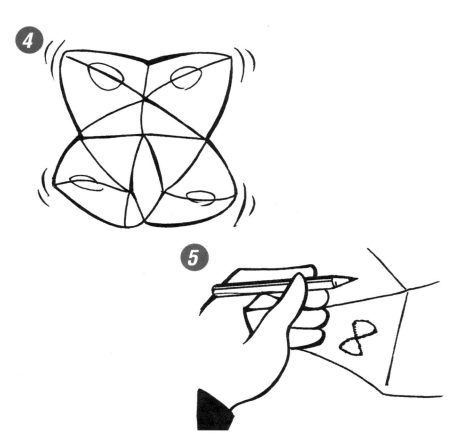

Don't show your friends. Write one under each small triangle.
Your fortune teller is ready. Tell a partner's fortune, like this:

– Choose a colour.

– Green.

– G - R - E - E - N.

(For each letter, open the teller alternate ways. Stop at the last letter, with the teller open.)

– Choose a number.

– 7.

– S - E - V - E - N.

(Do the same as above.)

– Choose another number.

– 3.

(Open the triangle and read the fortune under the number 3.)

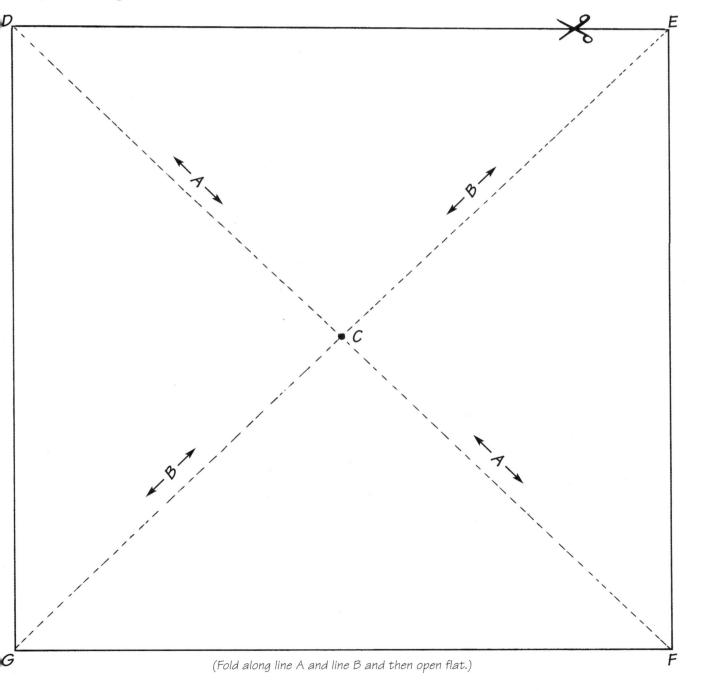

(Fold along line A and line B and then open flat.)

Alien Language

You and your friend Sam are out late one afternoon. It's just getting dark.
Suddenly a group of aliens appears in front of you. They speak in code.
Strangely, *you* can understand it, but Sam can't.

ALIEN CODE

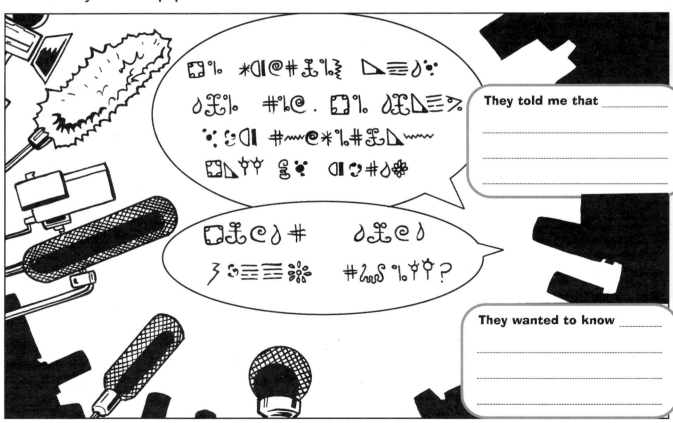

The next day the newspapers want to hear all about it. Tell them what the aliens said.

They told me that _____

They wanted to know _____

Imagine you are an alien visitor to the planet earth. What questions would you like to ask? Write
your questions in alien code. Exchange papers with a partner. Decode your partner's questions and
report them back to the class.

Towns and Villages

KEY

shop
swimming pool
cinema
health club
park
theatre
football club
playground
street market
art gallery
library
night club
restaurant
bar

Fill in the gaps with *a*, *some* or *any* and then decide where each person lives. Where do these people live?

MEGALOPOLIS

MAXICHESTER

MIDDOL

LITTLETON

Where I live, we've got _____ sports facilities, _____ cinema, _____ really good clothes shops and _____ lovely parks.

1. Emma lives in _____

We've got _____ cool street markets, _____ bar and the best football team in the world.

2. Ben lives in _____

There's _____ nice playground but we haven't got _____ shops.

3. Sky lives in _____

We love our town. We've got everything we want. There are _____ health clubs and a swimming pool. There are _____ nice playgrounds for our children. There's a bar where we can meet our friends. There aren't _____ night clubs which is good because we like peace and quiet.

5. Sally and Jim live in _____

I love art and reading. I hate football and shopping. I don't like my town very much. We've only got one cinema and we haven't got _____ theatres or art galleries. We've got _____ good street markets, though.

4. David lives in _____
He would prefer to live in _____

This is _ _ _ _ _ _ _ _ _

Check your answers and find the name of the most northerly capital city in the world.
Count how many of each word you used in the exercise.
Write the letters next to the correct numbers to find the city.

	1	2	3	4	5	6	7
some	Sto	Ams	Wel	Ven	Lon	Ber	Rey
any	ckh	kya	zur	don	ghe	phe	ter
a	ich	dam	vík	kyo	olm	ico	ris

Word Chain

1 Complete the name of the things in the pictures.
Use the words in the box to form compound nouns.

bag	friend	phone
book	glasses	pot
brush	hole	socket
clip	dream	switch
cup	lights	wheel

1 mobile _____

2 electric _____

3 text _____

4 key _____

5 egg _____

6 paper _____

7 plant _____

8 traffic _____

9 sun _____

10 steering _____

11 light _____

12 hair _____

13 hand _____

14 girl _____

15 day _____

Tropical Island

Some people arrived on a tropical island. A few weeks later they were rescued. Follow the sentence paths to read their story. When you choose between *some* and *any*, write the letter in the spaces at the bottom of the page to find out how they first arrived on the island.

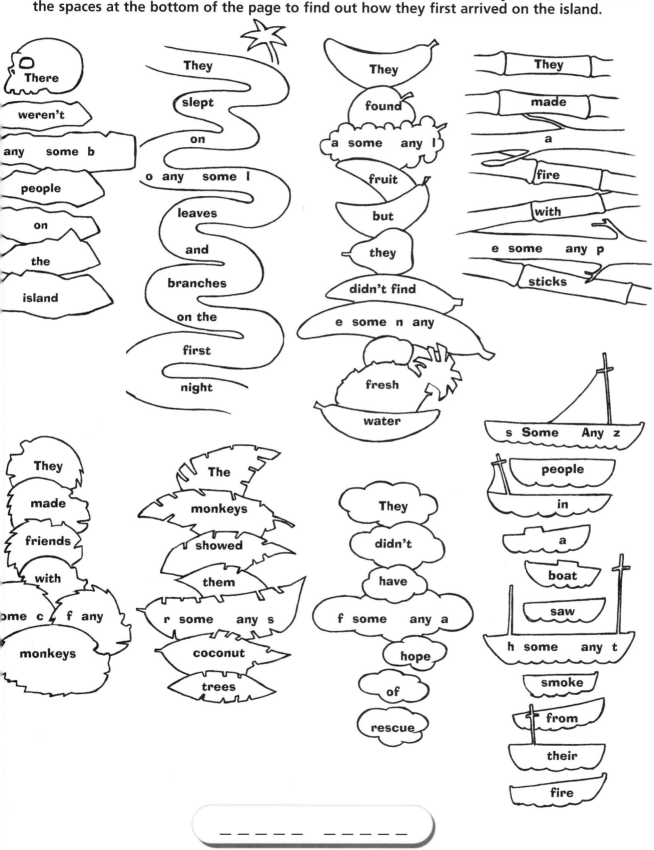

There weren't **any some b** people on the island

They slept on **o any some l** leaves and branches on the first night

They found **a some any l** fruit but they didn't find **e some n any** fresh water

They made a fire with **e some any p** sticks

They made friends with **ome c f any** monkeys

The monkeys showed them **r some any s** coconut trees

They didn't have **f some any a** hope of rescue

s Some Any z people in a boat saw **h some any t** smoke from their fire

_ _ _ _ _   _ _ _ _ _

2 Write the words in the word chain.
The last letter of a word is the first letter of the next word.

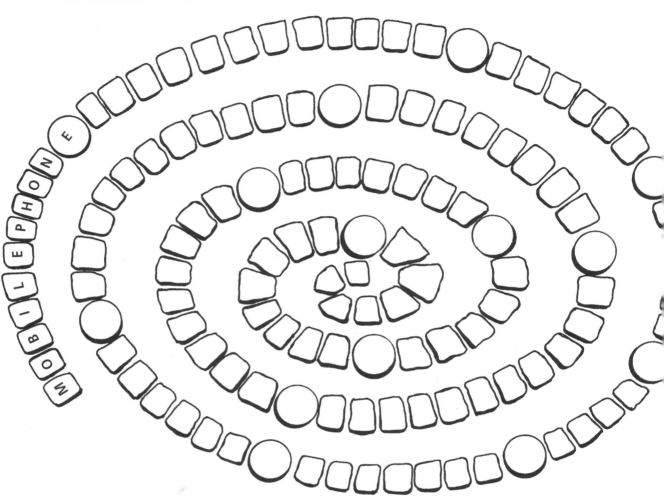

3 How many more compound nouns can you make?
Use the words in the box and continue the list.

school bag, address book, clothes brush,

This Creature is Weird

Look at the picture and fill in the missing words in the description below.

It has a tiger's [_____] , a chicken's [_____] , an elephant's [_____] and a peacock's [_____] .

	A	**B**	**C**	**D**
1				
2				
3				
4				
5				
6				
7				
8				
9				

GIRAFFE
PEACOCK
MONKEY
TORTOISE
ELEPHANT
FISH
PIG
SNAKE
EAGLE

HEAD
BODY
LEGS
TAIL

Draw and describe these weird creatures.

1 A6, B1, C9, D9   It _____

2 A3, B5, C7, D6   It _____

3 A9, B3, C1, D7   It _____

4 A8, B6, C4, D3   It _____

5 A7, B4, C2, D5   It _____

Draw your own creature.

Give your drawing to a partner.
He/She describes it to you. Is he/she right?

Lost Property

There's a queue at the Lost Property Office. Can you help the man match the people to their lost items? Write your answers in the sentences below.

1 They are the _____ toys.

2 It's the _____ map.

3 They are the _____ bones.

4 It's the _____ cheese.

5 It's the _____ pointed hat.

6 It's the _____ walking stick.

7 It's the _____ football.

8 They are the _____ hats.

City or Country?

What do city kids and country kids think about their lives?
Complete the speech bubbles with words from the box.

2 _____ plenty of open space.

There is _____ grass.

3 _____ not enough jobs.

There are _____ things to do in the evening.

5 There are _____ shops.

a lot of (I)   There is (F) not enough (F)   hardly any (Y) There are (T)

6 There is _____ concrete.

9 There are _____ cool shops.

0 _____ not enough clean air.

7 There are _____ places to ride our bikes.

8 _____ plenty of jobs.

hardly any (K)   There is (O)   too much (T)   plenty of (Y) There are (O)

Nearly _ _ _ _ _ per cent of the world's population live in cities and the largest city
           2 1 5 3 4
in the world is _ _ _ _ _ .
                  6 10 7 9 8

Which do you prefer?

life in the country ☐   life in the city ☐   Why? _____

These Clothes Don't Fit!

These children are all in the same class. The head teacher is checking their school uniform.

1 ....

2 ....

6 ....

4 ....

3 ....

5 ....

7 ....

3

2

4

5

6

7

1

Read what the head teacher says and write the correct name in the box next to each child.

Sam, your shirt is too scruffy!

Lara, your shoes are too tight!

Harry, your trousers are too short!

Emily, your skirt is too long!

Ned, your scarf is too long!

Geri, your boots are too big!

Isobel, your jacket is too small!

What is it?

Read the sentences. What does *one* or *ones* refer to in each sentence?

Harry has large round ones.

Isobel has a striped one.

Emily has black ones.

Ned has a striped one.

Sam has a large one.

Geri has white ones.

Lara has striped ones.

Is Anybody There?

Use the words in the box to complete the conversations.

> nobody   everybody   anybody   somebody
> nowhere   nothing   anywhere   somewhere

1

_____'s at the door.

2

Where is it?

It's _____ near here.

3

Who have you invited to this party?

_____!

4

You've got _____ to run to and _____ to hide.

Aaahhh!

5

Is _____ th-th-there?

6 Is there _____ to sit?

Yes, there are two seats here.

Sssssssshhhhhhhh!

7 _____ ever sends me an email!

8 What have you done with my newspaper?

_____.

Now find the next line of each conversation.

A Oh no! I'm going out, then.

B You get it!

C NNNNOOOOOOOOHHHHHHHHHH!

E You said that three hours ago!

D Maybe somebody's left a message on my mobile phone.

F Perhaps the dog ate it.

H But he has got a big brother.

G No, there aren't!

Now write the next line of each conversation. Show them to a partner. Can he/she match them to the conversations?

Street Market

We can say

or

> That girl has curly hair.

> That girl's hair is curly.

> frilly, spotty, glittery, plain, tall, short, flowery, stripy, big, little, spiky, curly, cheap, expensive, fat, thin, round, square

1 Look at these two street market scenes. There are nine differences. Circle the differences. Work with a partner. Take turns to describe a difference. Use the adjectives in the box to help you. Try to use the two different patterns.

2 Work with a partner. Choose something you would like to buy at this market. Don't tell your partner what it is.

Take turns. Describe your choice, like this.

It's small and spiky.

or *They're black leather.*

Can your partner find your choice?

Quick Quiz

How quickly can you find the answers to the following questions?

- What are they selling at the stall between the cafe and the T-shirt stall?

- What is on top of the TV building behind the canal?

- What is the man in the leather coat (with a big hat) counting?

- What is the bridge made of?

- What is sitting on the wall?

- What is going behind the clouds?

Write down the first letter of each thing you find.

Sort out the letters to find out where the two boys are going.

— — — — — —

Comparing Animals

a grey whale can be 15m long 	**an ostrich can run 65km/h** 	**a whale shark can be 18m long** 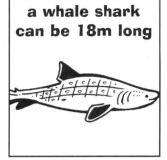	**a puma can jump 5m high** 
an African elephant can live 60 years 	**a Komodo dragon can be 3m long** 	**an Andean condor can weigh 12 kilos** 	**a giant squid can be 17m long** 
a cheetah can run 100 km/h 	**a bee hummingbird can weigh 1.4 grams** 	**a Mexican road-runner can run 45 km/h** 	**a polar bear can weigh 324 kilos** 
an albatross can live for 70 years 	**an emu can run 65 km/h** 	**a blue whale can weigh 155,963 kilos** 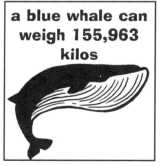	**an antelope can jump 3m high** 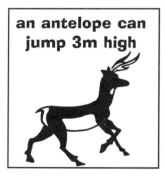
a blue whale can be 30m long 	**a dolphin can live for 60 years** 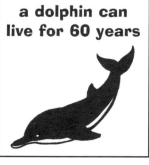	**a gazelle can run 90km/h** 	**a moose can weigh 362 kilos** 

Use the animal facts to help you decide if these sentences are true or false.

1 A bee hummingbird can weigh as much as a polar bear. **True** **False**

2 An African elephant can live just as long as a dolphin. **True** **False**

3 A polar bear can weigh nearly as much as a moose. **True** **False**

4 A cheetah can run twice as fast as a gazelle. **True** **False**

5 A Mexican road-runner can run half as fast as a gazelle. **True** **False**

6 A puma can jump higher than an antelope. **True** **False**

7 A whale shark can be a lot longer than a grey whale. **True** **False**

8 A giant squid can't be as long as a Komodo dragon. **True** **False**

Write some new animal facts using these phrases. Write some *true* facts and some *false* facts. Swap with a partner and try and decide which of your partner's sentences are true. Check your answers with the table.

1 as _____ as	_____
2 just as _____ as	_____
3 nearly as _____ as	_____
4 twice as _____ as	_____
5 half as _____ as	_____
6 -er than	_____
7 a lot -er than	_____
8 much -er than	_____

The Biggest and the Best!

These are some of the biggest, the highest, and the best in the world.
First label the pictures.

A. Angel Falls   **B. Sahara desert**   **C. banana spider**   **D. African elephant**   **E. Amazon River**
F. whale shark   **G. beetle**   **H. swift**   **I. Seismosaurus**   **J. koala bear**

Use the adjectives in the box to make superlatives about each picture.
Put them in the sentences below.

1 Angel Falls in Venezuela is the _____ waterfall in the world.

2 The Sahara is the _____ desert in the world.

3 The banana spider is the _____ there is.

4 The African elephant is the _____ animal on land.

5 The Amazon is the _____ river in the Americas.

6 The whale shark is the _____ shark in the oceans.

7 The beetle is the _____ insect in the world.

8 The swift is the _____ bird in the air.

9 The Seismosaurus was the _____ dinosaur on earth.

10 The koala bear is the _____ animal in the world.

heavy x2
large
sleepy
deep
common
high
deadly
fast

Careers Advisor

Choose the best career for each of these people.

> newspaper reporter   book editor   investment banker   airline pilot   doctor
> social worker   sports teacher   stunt performer   zoo keeper   vet

A

> I'm good at science. I'm not bad at talking to people. I'm good at mending things. I hate sports. I hate animals. I don't mind the sight of blood.

> I'm not very good at science and I'm very bad at practical tasks. I'm good at listening to people. I'm good at giving advice. I hate sports.

B

C

> I'm good at science. I'm not very good at meeting new people. I'm bad at writing. I love being outside. I hate sports. I love animals. I don't mind the sight of blood.

D

> I'm very good at science. I love animals. I'm good at meeting people. I don't mind the sight of blood.

> I'm bad at maths. I'm good at talking to people. I love travelling. I'm good at writing. I hate sports. I don't like animals. I don't mind the sight of blood.

E

F

> I'm good at English. I'm good at writing and checking details. I'm good at talking to people. I hate travelling.

G

> I'm good at maths. I'm good at writing. I'm good at making decisions. I like being inside. I hate sports. I don't like children. I hate the sight of blood.

H

> I'm good at science and maths. I'm good at languages. I love travelling. I hate staying in one place.

> I'm very good at team sports. I'm good at talking to young people. I love being outside. I'm good at biology but I'm bad at maths. I'm not very adventurous.

I

J

> I'm very good at sports especially extreme sports like sky-diving and bungee-jumping. I love animals. I'm not bad at drama.

At the Olympics

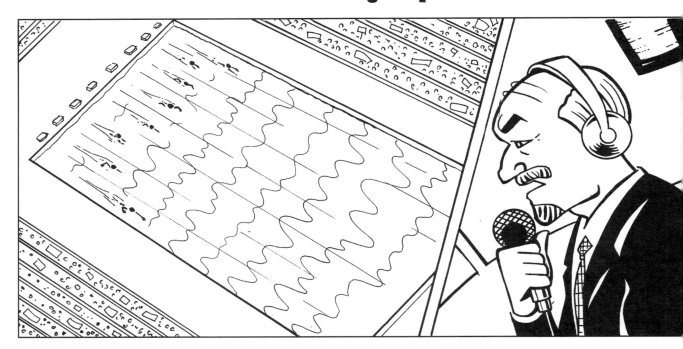

The adverbs in these sentences are mixed up. Put them in the correct sentences.

today	<u>Unluckily (o)</u> is another very exciting day at the Olympics.
	<u>Slowly (i)</u> we go to the Olympic swimming pool.
	<u>Extremely (o)</u> is the young swimmer that everybody is talking about.
	He swims as <u>today (t)</u> and as elegantly as a dolphin.
	<u>Ever (e)</u> for us, his race has just finished.
	But they are <u>first (h)</u> to begin the next race.
	Only three swimmers in this race. They're off! Oh no! A false start. Two of the swimmers dived in too <u>fast (t)</u>. They are disqualified. That leaves only one swimmer in the pool. Has this ever happened before?
	Off he goes. He seems to be swimming <u>apparently (s)</u> <u>early (t)</u>.
	<u>Here (e)</u> he has never swum in a 50-metre pool before. He only learned to swim a year ago
	Is he going to finish the race? Yes! In the slowest time <u>ready (r)</u>!

Write the letter attached to each adverb here:

T											

Which of these animals did the swimmer remind people of?

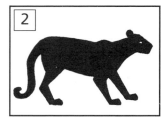

Robbie, the School Rabbit

Put *the* or *a / an* in the spaces in the story below.

Once upon (1) _____ time, on (2) _____ boring Wednesday
afternoon, Jed and Jen decided to steal Robbie, (3) _____ school rabbit. They
took it home. At (4) _____ time, they thought it was funny.
But (5) _____ next day, (6) _____ head teacher told (7) _____
whole school and everyone was very sad. Jed and Jen were sad, too.
"We'll have to put it back," said Jen. "But nobody must see us."

So that evening, they took (8) _____ rabbit back. They carried (9) _____
rabbit in (10) _____ box. At school there was (11) _____ evening class
going on, so (12) _____ school building was open. They crept in. They walked
quickly down (13) _____ main corridor. There were lots of doors into classrooms
and (14) _____ library. They turned the corner.

Suddenly they heard (15) _____ noise behind them - footsteps coming towards
the corner. They ran into (16) _____ classroom and hid. Jed put (17) _____
box down. They waited. (18) _____ footsteps walked away.
"Come on," whispered Jed. "Let's go."
"Oh no!" said Jen, too loudly. "(19) _____ rabbit's gone."

They rushed back into (20) _____ corridor. They were just in time to see
(21) _____ rabbit hop into (22) _____ main school hall. They ran to
(23) _____ hall but stopped suddenly. (24) _____ hall was full of
people speaking French. It was (25) _____ French evening class.

Did anyone see Jed and Jen? Did they get into big trouble? You write the end of the story.

Are You an Extrovert or an Introvert?

Read each opinion. Write your response in the AGREE or DISAGREE bubble underneath. Count up the faces attached to your answers. Ask your teacher for the analysis.

Choose your responses from here:

So do I. Neither do I. I wouldn t. I don t. I do. So would I.

Neither would I. I would. So am I. I m not.

1 I think riding my bike is more fun than watching TV.

AGREE _____ DISAGREE _____

2 I would rather do a bungee jump than make a speech in front of 100 people.

AGREE _____ DISAGREE _____

3 I would like to live in Hollywood.

AGREE _____ DISAGREE _____

4 I would rather be a famous TV star than a brilliant scientist.

AGREE _____ DISAGREE _____

5 I don't like going to big parties.

AGREE _____ DISAGREE _____

6 I wouldn't want to be a politician.

AGREE _____ DISAGREE _____

7 I'm only happy if I'm looking after animals.

AGREE _____ DISAGREE _____

8 I love practising my English with English speakers.

AGREE _____ DISAGREE _____

9 I like wearing really unusual clothes and having weird hair.

AGREE _____ DISAGREE _____

10 I prefer staying in to going out.

AGREE _____ DISAGREE _____

11 I only feel really happy in a room full of people.

AGREE _____ DISAGREE _____

Crazy World of Adventure

Henry went to the Crazy World of Adventure. He had £10 in his pocket.
Each ride cost £1. Read the information below and draw his route on the map.
Which rides did he go on twice? Which ride did he miss?

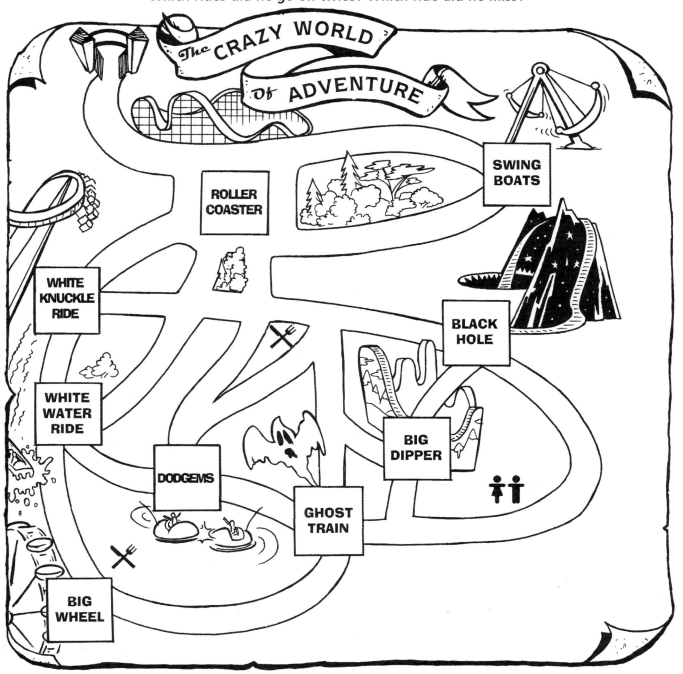

- First he went on the Rollercoaster.
- When he had £4 left, he went on the Rollercoaster again.
- Before he went on the Ghost Train, he went on the White Water Ride.
- After he went on the White Knuckle Ride, he went on Black Hole.
- The fifth ride he went on was the Big Dipper. After that, he went on the Dodgems.
- Last he went on Black Hole for the second time.
- Last but one, he went on the Ghost Train.
- He went on the Swing Boats second and then he went on the White Knuckle Ride.

Treasure Hunt

Follow the path to the treasure. Collect the letters on the way.

The first letter is **on** a straight path.

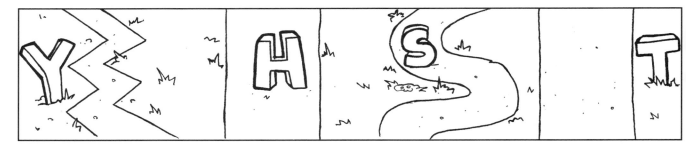

The second letter is **next to** a prickly bush.

The third letter is **in** a shark's mouth.

The fourth letter is **above** a triangular hole in the castle wall.

The fifth letter is **in front of** a narrow window halfway up a tower.

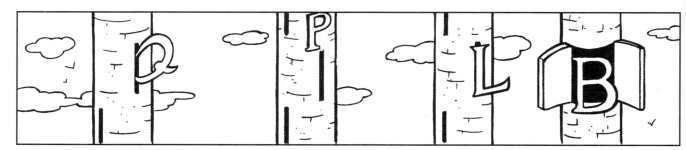

The sixth letter is **on top of** an octagonal tower.

The seventh letter is **behind** a tall, thin guard.

The eighth letter is **to the left of** a wooden box.

The ninth letter is **underneath** the striped cat.

Write your letters here. _ _ _ _ _ _ _ _ _

Sort them out to find the treasure. _ _ _ _ _ _ _ _ _

CLUE (The treasure will disappear quickly when you find it.)

Who Was First?

Eight runners ran a 100m race. Each runner wore a different shirt.
Use the information to work out the order they finished in. Draw the shirts.

I came in front of the runner in the spotted shirt.

I came in between the runner in the white shirt and the runner in the No.5 shirt.

I came behind the runner in the No.10 shirt.

I came after the runner in the spotted shirt but I came before five other runners.

I came before the runner in the black shirt.

I came in next to the runner in the No.10 shirt. Our times were exactly the same.

I came before the runner in the cat shirt.

I came behind the runner in the stripy shirt.

Who was first? Who was last? Draw their shirts.

Airport Journey

Janice and her mum are at the airport. They're going to visit Janice's grandparents.
Draw their route around the airport. Choose the right phrasal verbs as you go.
Pick up a letter at each symbol.

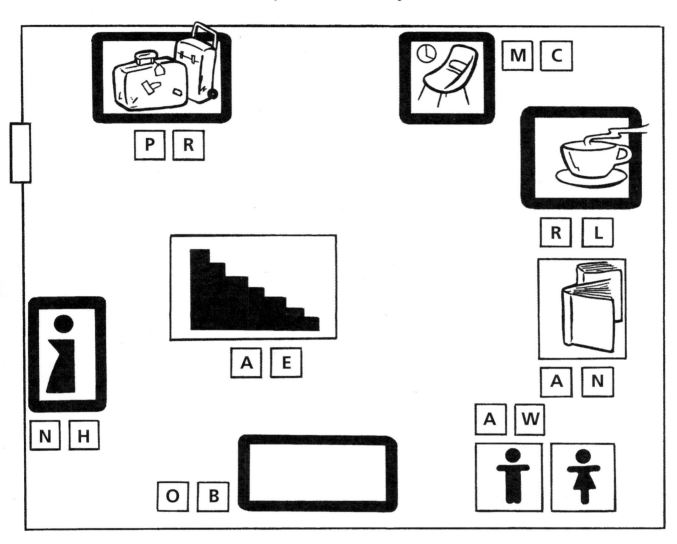

First they need to **1 find out / turn up** where their airline's desk is. They ask at the information desk (pick up the left-hand letter). They find the airline desk and **2 chuck out / check in** their heavy suitcases (pick up the right-hand letter). 'Now we have to **3 go up / swim across** to the first floor to the departures lounge (pick up the right-hand letter),' says Janice's mum. 'I need a coffee. Let's **4 look for / look up** a cafe.' 'There's one,' says Janice, pointing across the lounge (pick up the left-hand letter).

Later, Janice's mum wants to **5 look after / look at** some guidebooks, so they go to the bookshop (pick up the left-hand letter). But then Janice decides she needs to go to the toilet. So her mum **6 puts down / picks up** the guidebook she's reading, and off they go (pick up the left-hand letter).

Now they have half an hour to wait. 'Let's **7 sit down / stand up** in the waiting area,' says Janice's mum (pick up the right-hand letter). Soon they hear an announcement. "Flight 617 is now boarding at Gate 33." 'Great!' shouts Janice and they **8 run across / turn over** to their boarding gate (pick up the right-hand letter).

Now sort out your letters. Where are Janice and her mum going? _ _ _ _ _ _ _ _ _

Which country is it in? _ _ _ _ _ _ _ _ _

What's Happening?

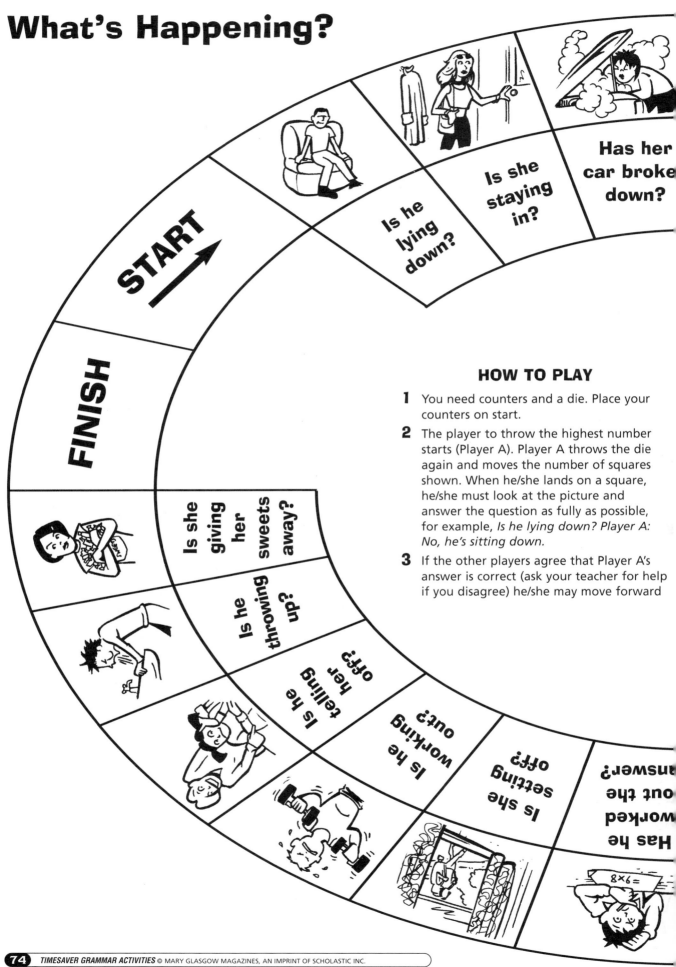

START

FINISH

Is he lying down?

Is she staying in?

Has her car broke down?

Is she giving her sweets away?

Is he throwing up?

Is he telling her off?

Is he working out?

Is she setting off?

Has he worked out the answer?

HOW TO PLAY

1 You need counters and a die. Place your counters on start.

2 The player to throw the highest number starts (Player A). Player A throws the die again and moves the number of squares shown. When he/she lands on a square, he/she must look at the picture and answer the question as fully as possible, for example, *Is he lying down? Player A: No, he's sitting down.*

3 If the other players agree that Player A's answer is correct (ask your teacher for help if you disagree) he/she may move forward

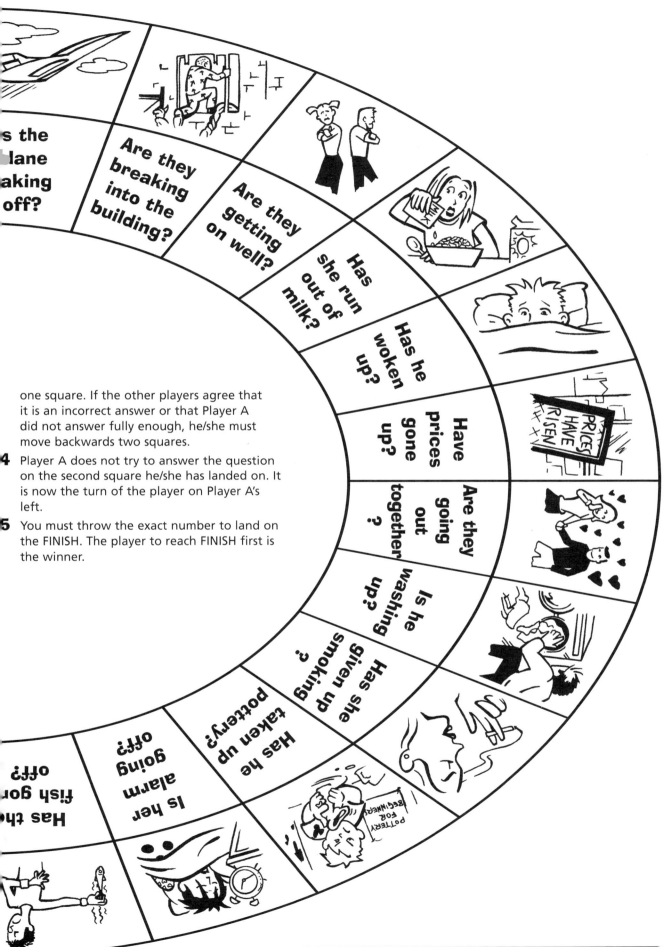

s the lane aking off?

Are they breaking into the building?

Are they getting on well?

Has she run out of milk?

Has he woken up?

Have prices gone up?

Are they going out together?

Is he washing up?

Has she given up smoking?

Has he taken up pottery?

Is her alarm going off?

Has the fish gone off?

one square. If the other players agree that it is an incorrect answer or that Player A did not answer fully enough, he/she must move backwards two squares.

4 Player A does not try to answer the question on the second square he/she has landed on. It is now the turn of the player on Player A's left.

5 You must throw the exact number to land on the FINISH. The player to reach FINISH first is the winner.

POTTERY FOR BEGINNERS

PRICES HAVE RISEN

PAGE 4   Who Are You?
Students complete this with information about themselves.

PAGE 5   Unchanging World
1. sleeps 2. sets 3. lasts 4. weighs, measures 5. loses
6. spends 7. throws, travels 8. drinks 9. closes 10. beats

PAGE 6   You're Late!
The verbs appear in this form, in this order: waiting, leaving, 'm sitting, 'm getting out, 'm going into, running, falling into, 'm getting on, 're driving down, 'm pushing, 'm running out of

*They are going to see **The Lion King***

PAGE 7   Where's Your Homework?
1. The dog ate it. 2. My computer exploded.
3. Some boys stole my school bag. 4. The queen came to tea.
5. Aliens landed in our garden and took my homework back to their planet. 6. An eagle took my homework and used it to make a nest. 7. My brother made a paper plane with it.
8. My father lit the fire with it. 9. A professor thought it was brilliant and took it back to his university. 10. Actually, ... (suggested answers) I forgot to do it/I watched TV all evening/I went out with my boyfriend/ here's my homework.

PAGE 8   Scary Stories
Story 1 Aliens landed on the earth. A boy with a hamburger heard their voices. 'Where are you?' he shouted. 'We are here. We are friendly. Help us,' they answered. He ate his hamburger. There was a loud crunch in his mouth.
Story 2 A group of ten adults and four children went to the island of Tunamo in the Pacific Ocean. Nobody lived there and they started a new society. Only giant spiders lived on the island. The spiders caught eight adults and four children in their web. The others escaped.
Story 3 A family lived on a windy hill. One night a bird sat outside the window and broke the glass. The next night there were hundreds of birds. The family couldn't get out. The birds were everywhere. They killed the family.

1. The boy killed the aliens. (they were in his hamburger) 2. The spiders killed the people on the island.
3. Two adults escaped. 4. The birds.

PAGE 9 Michael Johnson
1. broke 2. was 3. seemed 4. studied 5. realised 6. said 7. signed 8. won 9. retired

3)	S	E	E	M	E	D		
2)			W	O	N			
9) R	E	T	I	R	E	D		
1) B	R	O	K	E				
5)		R	E	A	L	I	S	E	D
4)		S	T	U	D	I	E	D
6)	S	A	I	D				
8) W	O	N						
7)	S	I	G	N	E	D		

*He studied **marketing**.*

PAGES 10 & 11   That's History!
1. Since 100,000 BC. 2. Since 20,000 BC. 3. Since 40,000 BC.
4. Since 4,000 BC. 5. Since 8,000 BC. 6. For 554 years.
7. For 177 years. 8. For 116 years. 9. For more than 90 years.
10. For more than 16 years.

PAGE 14   Here Is Today's News
1-f, 2-e, 3-h, 4-g, 5-a, 6-c, 7-d, 8-b

PAGE 15   Pompeii
1. He was drinking a glass of wine at the bar.
2. They were buying loaves and honey cakes.
3. They were playing a game with stones in the road.
4. She was writing a letter.
5. They were painting pictures of the countryside on the walls.
6. It was sleeping in the corner.
7. He grabbed Agrippina's hand and ran out of the house.
8. It hid under the table.
9. The children cried for their parents.
10. Most of them escaped but two thousand died.

PAGES 16 & 17   Memory Test
1. She was climbing a mountain.
2. He was having a shower.
3. They were swimming in the sea.
4. At 8.30 yesterday evening.
5. At 4.00 this afternoon.
6. She was riding a horse on the beach.
7. They were shopping.
8. At 4.00 this afternoon.
9. He was working on his computer.
10. He was ice-skating.

PAGE 18   A Fishy Story
1-b, 2-i, 3-c, 4-f, 5-h, 6-j, 7-a, 8-e, 9-g, 10-d.

PAGE 19   Amazon Diary
a-5, b-8, c-7, d-3, e-1, f-2, g-6, h-4

*He met four types of creature: **ants, piranha fish, a crocodile and a monkey.***

PAGES 20 & 21   Trip To Town
This is one possible plan
10.30 buy bread and cakes
          (remember the bakery sells out early)
10.45 post office (don't miss the 11 o'clock post)
11.00 bank (they shut at 12.00)
11.15 chemist (just time to buy shampoo and toothpaste)
11.30 hairdresser's
12.00 library
12.15 coffee with friends
1.00   Music/Video Megastore
1.30   shoe shop
2.00   go home

Page 22   What Is Going To Happen Next?
Possible answers:
The ants are going to steal/take the picnic.
The crocodile is going to eat the duck.
The bridge is going to break.
The swing is going to break.
The bull is going to push the woman over.
The monkey is going to steal/take the buns.
The newspaper is going to catch fire.
The little dog is going to steal/take the big dog's bone.

PAGE 23   Vote For Us
Yes: protect the countryside, create more jobs, build new, cheap houses
No: reduce crime, help farmers, prepare our young people for the future, modernise our transport system

PAGES 24 & 25   On Tour

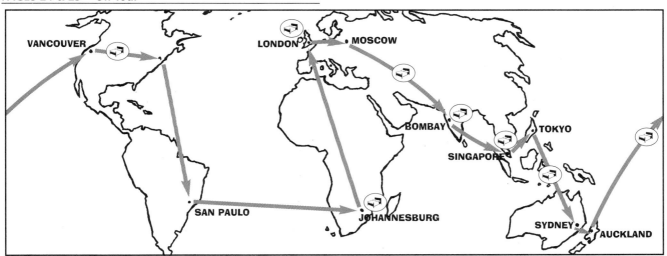

The name of the band is **Here Today**

PAGE 28   Emergency!

The correct answers:

1. a-4 He can pinch the top of his nose at the same time, b-0 that's for hiccups!, c-0
2. a-0 No! go straight outside, b-4, c-0
3. a-0 Don't touch it, b-4, c-0 It might be dangerous
4. a-0 It might bite you, b-0, c-4
5. a-0 The light switch can cause an explosion, b-4, c-0 Always report a smell of gas.
6. a-0, b-4, c-0
7. a-0 If it dries, it can't be put back in, b-4, c-4 You can try and put it back in yourself on the way to the dentist, but keep it WET.
8. a-2, b-4, c-0 The bleeding stops if you hold it up - get help as well
9. a-0, b-4, c-0
10. a-0, b-2 Some people think this works, c-2 Is there a cure for hiccups?

Your score:

0-20 I won't come to you in an emergency!
21-30 Pretty good score, but maybe you should take a Safety First or First Aid course.
31-40 Do you work for the emergency services?

PAGE 29   April Fool

1. If he opens the door, the flour will fall on his head.
2. If he looks in his desk, a frog will jump out.
3. If he sits down, he will stick to his chair.
4. If he writes on the board, the pen won't rub out.
5. If he plays the cassette, he will hear pop music.
6. If he opens his book, he will find a squashed tomato.
7. If he drinks his coffee, it will taste disgusting!

PAGE 30   What a Change!

(Possible sentences)

If this stapler came alive, it would look like a dog.
If this teapot came alive, it would move like an elephant.
If this hair clip came alive, it would run like a spider.
If this mouse came alive, it would look like a beetle.
If this pencil came alive, it would move like a snake.
If this toy car came alive, it would run like a monkey.

PAGE 31   What Kind of Artist Are You?

1. If you had half an hour to spare now, what would you do?
2. If you went to the theatre this evening, what would you choose to see?
3. If you went to see your favourite band this evening, what would you do in the half hour before you went?
4. If your English teacher asked you to choose a fun class activity, which one would you choose?
5. If these teachers met your parents, who would say the nicest things about you?
6. If you chose one person to represent America, who would you choose?

PAGE 32   A Tropical Island Is Born

is broken down, is trapped, are blown, is built up, is created, are replaced, is covered
Order of pictures: 1-e, 2-d, 3-f, 4-b, 5-a, 6-c.

PAGE 33   What's it Made of?

1	p	a	p	e	r			
2	m	e	t	a	l			
		3	p	l	a	s	t	i	c
4	s	t	o	n	e			
		5	r	u	b	b	e	r
		6	i	c	e			
7	w	o	o	l				
	8	b	r	i	c	k		
	9	r	o	p	e			
10	g	l	a	s	s			

It's made of paperclips.

PAGE 34   What Happened to You?

1. I've had my hair cut.
2. I've had my ears pierced.
3. I've had my hair dyed black.
4. I've had my car mended.
5. I've had my tooth taken out!
6. We've had our windows cleaned.
7. I've had my eyes tested.
8. I've had my face painted.

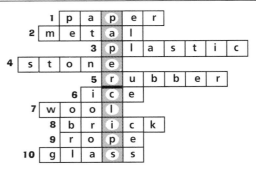

I've had my photograph taken.

PAGE 35   Great Natural Disasters

A 3/2/1: When Mt Vesuvius erupted in AD79, the Roman town of Pompeii was buried under a mountain of ash.

B 2/3/1: A fire started in Pudding Lane in London in 1666 and the city of London was burnt to the ground.

C 1/2/3: When the Titanic hit an iceberg in 1912, over 1,000 people were lost in the icy waters of the Atlantic Ocean.

D 2/3/1: In the Great Fire of 1871 in Chicago, the iron skyscrapers were melted to the ground by the heat.

E 3/2/1: After a terrible earthquake in Portugal in 1775, the city of Lisbon was hit by 15-metre-high waves.

PAGE 36   Zak's Coffee Bar

1. must, 2. mustn't, 3. mustn't, 4. must, 5. mustn't,
6. must, 7. mustn't, 8. must, 9. must, 10. must

Rules 1, 3, 4, 5 and 7 are being broken.

PAGE 38 & 39   The Rainbow Cafe

Table 1 - Bill 3

I'd like omelette and broccoli. What would you like?
I'd like a very healthy lunch - soup and salad.

Table 2 - Bill 4

I think I'd like a bowl of pea soup and a carrot and beetroot salad. How about you?
Okay. I'd like the same as you.

Table 3 - Bill 2

Would you like one, too?
No, I wouldn't, thanks.

Table 4 - Bill 1

Well, I'd like orange juice and a hamburger.
What would you like?

Bill 1 - Table 4; *Bill 2* - Table 3; *Bill 3* - Table 1; *Bill 4* - Table 2.

PAGE 40   School's Out

Alan a, Beth a, Chris b, Diana a, Ewan a, Flynn a,
Gill b, Harry a.

Chris and Flynn will need their swimming costumes.
(Gill, Ewan, Beth and Diana are going bowling. Alan and Harry are going to a cafe.)

PAGE 42   Our Bodies

1. to breathe, 2. to run
3. to stand up 4. to chew
5. to eat 6. to see 7. to balance
8. to write and draw
9. to store 10. to pump

A-5, B-9, C-6, D-4, E-10, F-1, G-3, H-8, 1-2, J-7.

PAGE 43   To:Ben@astro.co.uk

1. won't there? 2. will you? 3. can we? 4. doesn't she?
5. aren't you? 6. can't we? 7. can you?

The correct order is: c, g, e, j, b, f, a, i, d, h.

PAGES 44 & 45   Football Crazy

In A there is a pigeon on the goalpost - not in B.
In A the goalkeeper has a plain shirt, in B it is striped.
In A the referee is wearing glasses, but not in B.
In A the referee is blowing his whistle, but not in B.
In A the line official is holding up his flag, but not in B.
In A the ball is in the back of the net. In B the ball has just left the shooting player's foot.

In A the advert behind the goal is for Coca cola, in B it is for washing powder.
In A the sun is out, in B there are black clouds.
In A there is a flag above the stadium, in B there isn't.

PAGE 48   Alien Language

They told me that ... ... they had crashed their ship into the sea and that they thought that it would go rusty.
They wanted to know ... ... what the funny smell was.

PAGE 49   Towns and Villages

1. Megalopolis 2. Maxichester 3. Littleton
4. Megalopolis, Maxichester 5. Middol

This is *Reykyavik*

PAGE 50 & 51   Word Chain

1. mobile phone 2. electric socket 3. textbook 4. keyhole 5. egg cup 6. paper clip 7. plant pot 8. traffic lights
9. sunglasses 10. steering wheel 11. light switch
12. hairbrush 13. handbag 14. girlfriend 15. day dream

Note that some of these compound nouns are written as one word and others as two words.

PAGE 52   Tropical Island

The correct choices spell *plane crash*.

PAGE 53   This Creature is Weird

It has a tiger's head, a chicken's body, an elephant's legs and a peacock's tail.
1. It has a fish's head, a giraffe's body, an eagle's legs and an eagle's tail.
2. It has a monkey's head, an elephant's body, a pig's legs and a fish's tail.
3. It has an eagle's head, a monkey's body, a giraffe's legs and a pig's tail.
4. It has a snake's head, a fish's body, a tortoise's legs and a monkey's tail.
5. It has a pig's head, a tortoise's body, a peacock's legs and an elephant's tail.

PAGE 54   Lost Property

1. children's 2. aliens' 3. dogs' 4. mice's 5. magician's
6. old woman's 7. football players' 8. chefs'

PAGE 55   City or Country?

1. a lot of (I) 2. There is (F) 3. There are (T)
4. hardly any (Y) 5. not enough (F) 6. too much (T)
7. hardly any (K) 8. There are (O) 9. plenty of (Y)
10. There is (O)

Nearly fifty per cent of the world's population lives in cities and the largest city in the world is Tokyo.

PAGES 56 & 57   These Clothes Don't Fit!

1. Lara - trousers, 2. Emily - shoes, 3. Isobel - skirt, 4. Ned - scarf,
5. Sam - schoolbag, 6. Geri - socks, 7. Harry - glasses.

PAGES 58 & 59   Is Anybody There?

1. Somebody - B, 2. somewhere - E, 3. Everybody - A,
4. nowhere, nowhere - H, 5. anybody - C, 6. anywhere - G,
7. nobody - D, 8. Nothing - F.

PAGES 60 & 61   Street Market

In A a girl is wearing a frilly dress, in B it is spotty.
In A a girl is buying glittery jeans, in B they are plain.
In A a boy is short, in B he is tall.
In A a boy is wearing a flowery shirt, in B it is stripy.
In A a girl is buying a big bag, in B it is little.
In A a boy has spiky hair, in B it is curly.
In A you can buy three cheap tops for £2, in B you can buy three expensive tops for £45.
In A the dog is very fat, in B it is very thin.
In A the cat is wearing round sunglasses, in B they are square.

Quiz answers: noodles, eggs, money, iron, cat, aeroplane - CINEMA

PAGES 62 & 63   Comparing Animals

1, 4, 7, 8 are false.
2, 3, 5, 6 are true.

PAGE 64   The Biggest and the Best!

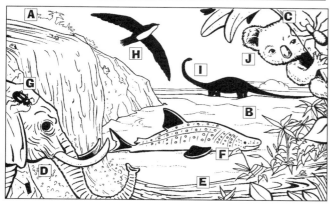

1. highest 2. largest 3. deadliest 4. heaviest 5. deepest
6. heaviest 7. commonest 8. fastest 9. biggest 10. sleepiest

PAGE 65   Careers Advisor

(Possible answers) A doctor B social worker C zoo keeper
D vet E newspaper reporter F book editor G investment
banker H airline pilot I sports teacher J stunt performer

PAGE 66   At the Olympics

Today (t) First (h) here (e) fast (t) Unluckily (o) ready (r) early
(t) extremely (o) slowly (i) apparently (s) ever (e)

The animal is 3 the tortoise

PAGE 67   Robbie, the School Rabbit

1. a 2. a 3. the 4. the 5. the 6. the 7. the 8. the 9. the
10. a 11. an 12. the 13. the 14. the 15. a 16. a 17. the
18. The 19. The 20. the 21. the 22. the 23. the 24. the
25. the

PAGE 68   Are you an Extrovert or an Introvert?

1. Agree: So do I. Disagree: I don't.
2. Agree: So would I. Disagree: I wouldn't.
3. Agree: So would I. Disagree: I wouldn't.
4. Agree: So would I. Disagree: I wouldn't.
5. Agree: Neither do I. Disagree: I do.
6. Agree: Neither would I. Disagree: I would.
7. Agree: So am I. Disagree: I'm not.
8. Agree: So do I. Disagree: I don't.
9. Agree: So do I. Disagree: I don't.
10. Agree: So do I. Disagree: I don't.
11. Agree: So do I. Disagree: I don't.

Analysis

Count up your happy faces.

11-16 Definitely an introvert. You are an inward-looking person. You prefer your own company or one or two friends to big crowds. You prefer to spend your time in non-social situations. You probably like indoor and outdoor activities, but you don't like a crowd of people looking at you.

17-23 You like friends and you like your own company. You are quite confident in social situations and not afraid of them. You are not shy but you are not an extrovert either.

24-33 You want to stand out from the crowd. You also need the crowd's approval. Socially you seem very confident, but secretly you may be less confident about yourself. You have lots of friends and always attract a lot of attention. You feel a failure if you find yourself at home on your own on a Saturday evening.

PAGE 69   Crazy World of Adventure

Route: the Rollercoaster, the Swing Boats, the White Knuckle Ride, the Black Hole, the Big Dipper, the Dodgems, the Rollercoaster, the White Water Ride, the Ghost Train, the Black Hole.

The Rollercoaster and the Black Hole

He didn't go on the Big Wheel.

PAGES 70 & 71   Treasure Hunt

The treasure is *chocolate*

PAGE 72   Who Was First?

1st: striped shirt, 2nd: spotted shirt, 3rd: zig-zag shirt,
4th: white shirt, 5th: black shirt, 6th=: No.5 shirt,
6th=: No.10 shirt, 8th: cat shirt

PAGE 73   Airport Journey

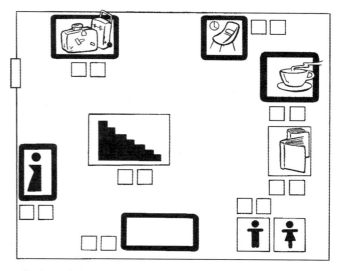

1 find out (N) 2 check in (R) 3 go up (E) 4 look for (R) 5 look
at (A) 6 puts down (A) 7 sit down (C) 8 run across (B)

They are going to Canberra, Australia

Material written by: Jane Rollason

Editors: Emma Grisewood and Jane Myles

Designer: Alison Bond/Bondi Design

Cover Photo: Christopher Woods/MOT Models

Cover Design: Kaya-anne Cully

Illustrations by: Carl Flint

Photo: (Page 9) Wally Mcnamee / Corbis

Mary Glasgow Magazines, an imprint of
Scholastic Inc., 2002

Printed in the UK by Ashford Colour Press Ltd.